HOW TO BECOME A MILLIONAIRE IN YOUR CURRENT JOB

CHOOSE WISELY WITH 401(k) AND IRA

J. B. Davis, MBA, CFP

Galaxy Publishing Co.

Galaxy Publishing Co., P.O. Box 10035, Houston, TX 77206

Printed in the United States of America
10 9 8 7 6 5 4 3 2 1   1 2 3 4 5 6 7 8 9 10

**Publisher's Cataloging-in-Publication
(Provided by Quality Books, Inc.)**

Davis, J. B. (Jackson B.)
How to become a millionaire in your current job :
choose wisely with 401(k) and IRA / J.B. Davis.
-- 1st ed.
p. cm.
Includes index
LCCN: 99-94278
ISBN: 0-9670511-4-2

1. Finance, Personal. 2. 401(k) plans.
3. Individual retirement accounts. 4. Retirement--
United States--Planning. 5. Investments.   I.
Title.

HG179.D38 1999   332.024'01
                        QBI99-543

Attention: Business Owners, Gift Givers, Personnel Managers, Financial Planners, and Schools. Quantity discounts are available on bulk purchases of 10 or more copies of this book. Custom imprinting or book excerpts can also be created to fit specific needs. For information, please see ordering instructions at the back of this book, visit our Internet site at www.401kmillionaire.com, write the publisher at the above address, or call 1-800-338-7153.

ACKNOWLEDGMENTS

I thank my friends who took the time to review the manuscript and helped me improve it: my daughter Shannon Peairson, John McCall, Ernie Kacher, Cynthia Torrance, Jim Shaw, Mia Jattuso and Alice Simms. Alice also put many hours into helping create the graphs and tables.

My editor, Sheila Brockmeyer of Roanoke Virginia, did a truly outstanding job. Thanks to her recommendations, I cut some parts of the manuscript and greatly simplified the explanations in other sections of the book.

Credit for the excellent cover design goes to a very talented artist and calligrapher who is also my wife, Susan Davis. Many thanks to Susan for the cover and for her patience in waiting for this book to be finished.

This publication is designed to provide accurate and authoritative information in regard to the subject matter covered. It is sold with the understanding that neither the author nor the publisher is engaged in rendering legal, accounting, or other professional service. If legal advice or other expert assistance is required, the services of a competent professional person should be sought.

—From a Declaration of Principles, jointly adopted by a Committee of the American Bar Association and a Committee of Publishers.

CONTENTS

CONTENTS

CONTENTS

WHO SHOULD READ THIS BOOK?

This book is written primarily for people who are living from paycheck to paycheck and whose highest goals are something other than the accumulation of great wealth! It's for people in ordinary occupations: accountants, clerks, engineers, factory workers, mechanics, nurses, secretaries, small business owners, technicians, tradesmen, etc. You can work hard and achieve great wealth or you can work hard and never get ahead financially. The choice is largely yours to make.

Generally, there are four legal ways to become wealthy. Earn it, win it, inherit it, or marry into it. Most people are not going to earn huge incomes, marry into wealth, or inherit it. The only way left for most people seems to be to win the lottery. That thinking is part of the reason lotteries are so popular! However, you don't have to win the lottery. Most young graduates of trade school, high school, and college can accumulate $1,000,000. Little is required.

The purpose of this book is to provide easy-to-understand, comprehensive information on how you can achieve financial independence and security. I will cover reasons to use a plan and barriers to even starting one. The book explains how to easily reduce expenses, save money, and safely invest your money. You will learn more than just the facts. You will also learn the very important emotional aspects of both saving and investing. The book covers new developments, including the Roth IRA and the SIMPLE IRA for small businesses.

If you're already investing in 401(k) or IRA accounts, you can learn how to increase your performance, reduce your investment risks, or both. Those of you already contributing the maximum to your 401(k) plan can skip Chapters 1, 2, 4, and 5. However, everyone should read Chapter 3. Information on page 31 of Chapter 3 could save you hundreds of thousands of dollars, regardless of what investments you have in your 401(k) or IRA.

The language and technical topics in this book are directed to financial novices as well as to other people who already have a good understanding of risk and investments.

Using the principles covered in these pages can be very profitable. People in their 40s and 50s can get good results. The best benefits will be achieved by young people in their 20s and 30s who have full-time jobs. This is not a get rich quick opportunity. So the more time you have, the better the results can be. The general principles of this book are quite simple. All you have to do is save a small portion of your income each year and invest that money with minimum risk into 401(k) and/or IRA plans in order to achieve substantial wealth after taxes and inflation.

One reason there are not more millionaires is that intelligent people in most occupations have not been given the knowledge of how to do it. In addition, they imagine it would be too hard or require too much self sacrifice. This book gives you the knowledge you need and shows how you can achieve your goals easily. After reading this book, you will have the knowledge and motivation to make a decision which could mean the difference between future prosperity and hard times.

Nothing in life is guaranteed except death and taxes. There is no guarantee that following the principles in this book will result in $1,000,000 for you. Nevertheless, based upon sound principles and many years of successful experience, you have a good chance to achieve great wealth by following the simple guidelines described here.

CHAPTER 1

WHY BOTHER TO BE WEALTHY?

Wealth Improves Your Life

Whatever your personal beliefs and life goals are, great wealth can substantially improve your life. Even if you don't want wealth for yourself or your children, giving a substantial amount of money to your favorite charity could provide help to others and joy for yourself.

Certainly, $1,000,000 constitutes wealth. But what is financial wealth? What does financial wealth mean to you? It doesn't have to mean being a workaholic or being obsessed with money. It doesn't have to mean that money is more important than people. It does mean the material things or services you can buy for yourself, your family, or others. It can mean exotic vacations, a beautiful home, school tuition for your children, financial independence, a substantial gift to your favorite charity, and much more.

What would you want if you had $1,000,000? Take a few minutes to describe what you want in writing. Where is your new home? What kind and color of new car or boat do you want? How will you get to your vacation destination? How often will you eat at your favorite restaurant? What will you buy for your children? What will your favorite charity do with your donation? These benefits can be yours by successfully applying the principles in this book.

What I would do with $1,000,000 or with the earnings on $1,000,000:

1.

2.

3.

4.

5.

According to the government, Americans are now living longer than ever before. Life expectancy when Social Security began in 1935 was 64 years for women and 59 for men. Today it is about 80 for women and 73 for men. You certainly don't want to run out of money, even at age 80. Fifty percent of Americans live beyond age 85, and 10 percent of us live to 93.

Thanks to better nutrition, exercise, and medical treatment, we can be very healthy and active for most of or all of our lives. Recent research studies have documented improved lifestyles for seniors. Most seniors are now healthy and active well into their 80s. They're enjoying a very active lifestyle for 20 or 30 years after normal retirement age. For those just now graduating from school, the norm may be good health into your 90s. The future is indeed bright for those who will be financially prepared for it. On the other hand, by not following these principles, you run a much greater risk of suffering financial problems both before and after retirement.

Well paying jobs are not as secure as they once were, and lifetime employment with a single employer is becoming rare. Therefore, you are much more likely to need a nest egg during your working years in order to avoid or reduce the problems of unemployment or underemployment.

Social Security's Big Problem

After retirement, the financial situation of the unprepared is likely to be even more precarious. For good reasons, today's young people don't expect much for themselves from Social Security. Social Security operates as a pay-as-you-go system. Benefits to recipients come not from their own contributions, but from taxes on current wage earners. This type of system critically depends on the support ratio – the number of workers in comparison to the number of beneficiaries. That support ratio continues to decline dramatically. In the 1930s, it was 30 to one. In 1950, there were 16 workers per beneficiary. Today there are only three workers for each beneficiary. As the huge baby boom generation retires, the ratio is expected to drop below two to one.

The current system simply cannot be as generous in the future as it has been in the past. There are three basic ways to keep the system going in the future: increase the retirement age, increase taxes, and decrease benefits. The projected future deficits are so huge that most likely all three methods will have to be used. No political party can change the basic problem, the ratio of workers to beneficiaries. However, politicians can postpone the inevitable. Unfortunately, the more successful they are in postponing needed changes, the more painful the changes will be when they come.

Think Again About Your Company's Pension Plan

If you work for a large employer, there is a good chance your employer has a pension plan. You don't have to contribute anything to the plan, and the plan takes care of you when you retire. So why bother to be wealthy at age 50 or 65? Even if Social Security benefits are not as good in the future as they were in the past, you've still got the company pension plan. There's no real need for anything else, right? Hardly! Certainly, a company pension plan is a good thing, but how much reliance you can put on it? The philosophy of most of the corporate pension plans goes way back to the time when life expectancy after retirement was significantly shorter than it is now. At that time, the plans didn't need to be very generous. In the 1990s, these plans have serious limitations for most workers.

The first problem is vesting. Vesting means entitled to benefits. Typically, you have to work for the company for several years before becoming vested. Many workers change jobs so frequently that they never become vested in any pension plan. So, if you don't really know how long you'll be with the same company, it's only prudent to rely on your own savings.

The second limiting problem is that the formulas used to calculate benefits are based on years of service. Typically, the formulas are set up to provide upon retirement at age 65 a certain percentage of your ending salary. That percentage is based on your working there 30 years or so. Those who become vested but do not stay for 30 years will get proportionally lower benefits.

The next limiting factor is what's called Social Security integration. Most large pension plans have this feature. The company reasons that since it pays FICA (Social Security taxes) on employees' wages, the company retirement benefit should be adjusted downward accordingly. Every paycheck stub you get shows a deduction for social security taxes. The employer pays your withheld amount plus an equal amount from company funds to the government. In other words, your employer pays 50% of the total social security taxes. Therefore, the retirement benefits calculation typically reduces your pension to take into account the fact that the company has provided half of your social security contribution.

That arrangement seems fair enough. But the problem is that it favors highly paid employees. Social security taxes are not collected on all employees' wages. The tax is figured on wages up to a certain maximum amount, which changes each year. As of 1998, the maximum social security tax wage was $68,400. Wages above that amount are not subject to the tax. Typically, company benefit formulas favor employees earning more than the social security wage base.

One more problem with most company pension plans is that they provide a fixed monthly benefit. Some pension plans have a COLA (cost of living adjustment) provision to increase the monthly benefits for inflation. Most plans do not have a COLA. The value or purchasing power of a fixed pension can be substantially eroded over a ten or twenty-year period.

Most large corporations realize that the old style pension plan is inadequate. More is needed for a decent retirement. Fortunately, many large corporations have added a new plan to meet the needs of their employees. As you probably already know, most of the new plans are based on section 401(k) of the Internal Revenue Code. These 401(k) plans can provide substantial wealth.

Keep Your Options Open

Many people have a hard time visualizing a successful future. After all, if your past has been difficult or painful, why expect anything different in the future? Why should you spend any time at all planning for the future?

Certainly, Jane feels that way. Jane is a 23-year-old single working woman. She has been telling her good friend Martha how she feels about saving for the future. "Becoming a millionaire is a fantasy, a Hollywood movie," she says. "My parents and everybody I know live paycheck to paycheck. The long-term future is bleak. You get old, have less money, pinch pennies, and then die. I don't want to even think about it. Frankly, I'd feel guilty if I had a lot more money than my parents. I don't want to scrimp and save for the rest of my life. I would rather marry a rich man than save my own money."

"Let's face it, Martha. I don't have a college degree in Finance, and I'm not an expert on how to invest money. If I could save any money, which I can't, I'd probably lose it in bad investments. I think the best idea is to spend everything I make and let tomorrow take care of itself."

Certainly, Jane has some psychological barriers to becoming a millionaire. At the same time that Jane is holding these views, it's important for her to realize that change is possible. The future doesn't have to be like the past. You don't have to believe that change is likely, only that it's possible. Once you can say it's possible, then don't close out the possibility. Keep your options open. Don't limit yourself. It may or may not happen for you, but don't close the door on it.

This book is written for Jane as well as for highly motivated accountants and lawyers who are already investing in IRAs and 401(k)s (explained in Chapter 3). Now, let's consider some of the issues Jane raised in her discussion with Martha. The first point is that almost everyone seems to live paycheck to paycheck. Certainly, you can't save money and become a millionaire if you're living in that situation, can you? Actually, a huge number of people are doing it right now. The secret is to pay yourself first, as explained in Chapter 4.

Jane doesn't want to think about the future. Unfortunately, fear of the future becomes a self-fulfilling prophecy because fear holds you back from taking positive steps. Unless you take those positive steps to achieve financial security, the future does become bleak. In order for your long-term future to be bright, it is important to start taking short-term steps now. The first step could be as simple as saving your spare change each day for a few months or saving for your next vacation.

Jane believes she would feel uncomfortable with far more money than her parents. Realize that almost all parents want their children to be successful. There's no need to feel guilty because your parents didn't have the opportunity to invest in an IRA or 401(k) when they were young. Furthermore, your feelings will most likely change by the time you become a millionaire. Nobody except you needs to know how much money you have. If you want to provide financial support to your parents when they get older, you'll be able to do so.

Jane doesn't want to save money. She wants to marry into money or get a sudden windfall, such as a lottery jackpot. Everybody has such fantasies. It's only natural and fun. However, the fantasy could be a barrier to getting the results you want. The fantasy can be an excuse for doing nothing for yourself. If the fantasy comes true, so much the better. But if it doesn't, you need to take care of yourself by saving and investing for your future. You keep your options open by starting a savings plan now, not later.

You don't need to have a degree in Finance. You don't need to be a money expert. You don't even need to be out of debt to make this program work. Just keep an open mind and commit to this program for one year. After one year, decide how easy or hard it will be to keep with it a second year and so on.

CHAPTER 2

I WANT TO BE WEALTHY PROVIDED THAT . . .

So, if great wealth is good, why do so few people attempt to achieve it – except through lotteries and gambling? Another way of expressing this is:

I Want to Be Wealthy Provided that . . .

- I Won't Have to Sacrifice Now for Future Benefits.
- There Is No Risk of Losing Any Part of My Savings.
- There Are No Risks of Any Losses.
- It Doesn't Take Too Much Hard Work.
- I'm Still Young Enough to Enjoy it.
- People Remain More Important to Me Than Money.
- My Relatives Don't Hound Me to Death for "Loans."
- My Friends Don't Become Envious and Leave Me.
- Nobody is Harmed by My Success.
- It Doesn't Take Away Too Much Time From My Family.
- It Doesn't Spoil My Children.
- I Can Still Be My Own Person.
- Money Management Does Not Stifle My Creativity.
- It Doesn't Harm My Spirituality.

What are your "provided thats"? Take a few minutes now to write down your personal list, including any not mentioned above.

I want to be wealthy provided that:

1.

2.

3.

4.

5.

6.

The "provided thats" are actually other goals which appear to be in competition with the goal of wealth. At first glance some of the above "provided thats" appear to be in direct contradiction to the stated goal of future wealth. Each statement must be analyzed to determine if the two goals are truly in contradiction. For the overwhelming majority of people, even the seemingly contradictory goals can be reconciled through some compromise. Let's look at each of the examples above to examine the process of reconciling competing goals.

I want to be wealthy provided that I don't have to sacrifice in the present in order to possibly benefit in the future. This is a tough one. Some people will not be able to reconcile these goals and thus not fully benefit from this book. Most people can reconcile the two goals. There are several ways you can do it.

First, would you be willing to make a small investment on the chance of gaining, say, 15 times your original outlay? Depends on the chance of success, right? Let's say that based on one hundred investments, your theoretical or expected outcome would be a $15 return ninety out of a hundred times, a $1 return on eight out of a hundred times, and $-0- on two times out of a hundred. In chart form, the above example is described as follows:

Probability	Expected return
90%	$15
8%	$1
2%	$-0-

Most people would take the chance of gaining $15 on a $1 investment if the odds for success were as described above. If you were unlucky enough to lose your $1, you would indeed have lost or sacrificed in the present in order to possibly benefit in the future. So, it looks like compromise may be possible for most people in reconciling the two seemingly contradictory goals.

The above example becomes more interesting by adding 000s. Would you spend $1000 in a chance to gain $15,000 if the odds were as stated above? Probably so, if you could easily afford the $1000. If you had $2000 and had not taken a vacation all year, you might go on a $1000 vacation and take the risk with the other $1000. In that event, chances are 90% you would have $15,000 for future vacations.

What does all that have to do with the real world? In the real world you can invest $1000, and it can grow to $15,000 over time due to compound interest or compound growth. $1000 invested at 12% earnings per year accumulates to $15,179 at 24 years. Of course, risk, price inflation, taxes, time required, and estimated rate of increase are important factors, which will be covered in later chapters.

I mentioned earlier that there are several ways to reconcile the goals of saving for the future and not wanting to make present sacrifices. The first way is to compromise and be willing to sacrifice a little bit. However, you may be unwilling to risk lowering your standard of living by even a penny. Can the two goals be reconciled under that tough position? Possibly so.

What if you were able to utilize some of the money saving ideas in Chapter 5 to save $1000, without lowering your standard of living? Say you could purchase all of the same goods and services for $1000 less than you're paying now. If you would be willing to save and invest even a small portion of that $1000, you would reconcile your two goals. What if you received a year-end bonus of $1000? Once again, if you were able to save and invest some of that $1000, your two goals would be reconciled to that extent. You could save money and not reduce your current standard of living.

What if you could get a pay raise from your employer by saving a little bit each month? Many people work for corporations which offer 401(k) plans for their employees. Many of these plans offer the employees a pay raise in the form of matching contributions to these plans. Do you really want to turn down that pay raise? Are you sure you won't need the accumulated balance of that pay raise at some time in the future?

If you're living paycheck to paycheck, as most people are, you may think it's impossible to save anything. Next time you get a pay raise, put half of the pay raise into the company 401(k) plan. For example, let's say you make $1000 per month and the company has a 100% matching contribution plan. At your job review, you get a raise to $1060 per month, a 6% raise. You direct the company to put $30 per month into the plan. Your gross take home pay before taxes goes from $1000 to $1030. The company matches your $30 in the savings plan; so you actually get a $60 contribution to the plan. Your total raise was as follows:

> $30 increase in gross take home pay (before taxes)
> $30 which you contributed to the 401(k) plan
> <u>$30</u> company contribution to the plan
> $90 Total

Since your gross take home pay increases by $30 in this example, the sacrifice of saving the other $30 is virtually painless. More will be said throughout the book on the "sacrifice of saving."

Depending on what compromises you are willing to make, you may be able to save and invest for future wealth without sacrificing your current standard of living. Of course many people are willing to make a small sacrifice in their current standard of living in order to provide for future needs. Whatever you decide, it's a personal choice without a right or wrong answer.

I want to be wealthy provided that there is no risk of losing any part of my savings. Many people are afraid of investment risks without having an understanding of what those risks actually are. Risk is not a simple concept in this context, but you should be able to understand it by the time you finish this book. There are four aspects of investment risk: loss of principal, loss of purchasing power, fluctuation in value, and financial or intrinsic value risk. In this section, we'll introduce the first two aspects of risk.

Many people have a fear of failure. Losing all of your savings on a bad investment could certainly be considered a failure. Even losing a small portion of your savings could be considered a failure. So, if you don't want to risk a loss or a failure, can you reconcile or compromise your goals? Can you accumulate wealth and not risk failure at the same time? The short answer is yes. Most people reconcile these two goals by putting their savings into investments insured by the FDIC (Federal Deposit Insurance Corporation). Typically, the investments are CDs (certificates of deposit) at a bank insured by the FDIC. There's nothing wrong with CDs. Different investments have different advantages and disadvantages. The disadvantage of CDs is that these relatively safe investments tend to have low rates of return.

Consider this modification of investing all your savings into CDs in order to avoid any risk of failure. Let's say you could afford to put $1000 per year into savings. Not wanting to risk any loss, you put the $1000 into a one year CD paying 6% interest. At the end of the first year you have $1060, of which $60 is income. Instead of investing the balance of $1060 into a CD for the next year, you could reinvest $1000 into a CD and put the $60 into a second investment with a greater risk and potentially greater rate of earnings. Each year you would invest all the earnings into the second investment. Over a period of years, the combination of these two investments would likely grow significantly faster than an investment in CDs only. If the second investment grew at 12% compounded annually, the result would be substantially better.

Over a 25-year period, you invest $25,000 out of pocket, in each case in the above example. In both cases, you have eliminated the risk of losing any of your original savings because you have invested in FDIC insured CDs. Even if you lost everything in the secondary investment, you would still have your original $25,000. Losing everything in the secondary investment is not even a realistic possibility with proper diversification to reduce risks. We'll cover diversification later in this book.

In the above example, the additional gains are hardly significant in the first several years. However, over a period of twenty-five years, compound growth produces a dramatic difference of $30,251 ($88,406 - $58,155). The complete table showing year by year results is included in Appendix A at the back of this book. Small adjustments in investment strategy can yield tremendous additional benefits over a long period of time. In summary, this combination of investments approach can enable you to increase your wealth without the risk of losing any of your out-of-pocket investment.

Although federal insurance guarantees against loss of principal, nothing guarantees against the second risk − loss of purchasing power. During most years, prices for goods and services increase slightly. Over a long period of time, annual increases in prices of goods and services substantially reduce the value of a fixed number of dollars. For example, a restaurant meal which cost $2 in 1960 may cost $8 today. Thus the $2 you saved in 1960 is worth only ¼ as much today compared to 1960. In order to maintain purchasing power or value of your money, your investments need to produce gains as fast as the rate of inflation. Ideally, you want the investment gains to be greater than the rate of inflation so that you can purchase more goods and services in the future than you can purchase now.

The FDIC insured CD substantially eliminates the risk of loss of principal. However, in some years for some taxpayers, CDs have caused the investor to lose purchasing power of his or her investment. If price inflation is 4%, interest on CDs is 5%, and the investor is in the 28% tax bracket, the investor is losing purchasing power. In this example, income taxes reduce the 5% interest income by 28% After taxes, the interest income is 3.6%, compared to 4% inflation. So, he or she has the choice of accepting a sure loss in purchasing power or trying to increase the purchasing power by investing in assets not guaranteed by the FDIC. In a sense, the investor is caught between a rock and a hard place, regardless of how he or she feels about risk.

I want to be wealthy provided that there are no risks of any losses. Even FDIC insurance has a very small risk of failure. Since all savings and investments have risk, the obvious conclusion is to save nothing. However, running away from investment risks actually causes other related risks to increase. If you're living paycheck to paycheck, you risk the financial consequences of losing your job. Without some savings, you may be in immediate danger of losing your belongings if you owe money to creditors. You could be forced into bankruptcy.

At some point, you will need to retire from your job. Without some of your own savings, you are dependent upon your employer's pension, if any, plus Social Security and other government assistance. Since the beginning of the Social Security system in 1934, the government has been extremely generous to its beneficiaries. Demographic and financial factors will almost inevitably reduce, possibly drastically, the government's ability to provide generous benefits by the year 2015 and beyond. Without the advantage of your own savings, you risk a substantial decrease in your future standard of living. Risks exist. There is no way to completely avoid risk. What we can do is manage or diminish risks by making prudent decisions.

I want to be wealthy provided that it doesn't take too much hard work. Actually, the hard work consists in getting and keeping a good job. That's all. Hopefully, the pay scale for your occupation will enable you to set aside for yourself a small amount each month or each year. You may think that's too hard, due to the fact that you're in debt and living from paycheck to paycheck with nothing to spare. With some planning and some discipline this problem can usually be overcome with much less sacrifice that you may think. In fact, you may even be able to enjoy this part of the plan. More on that in Chapter 5.

After you have that good job, there's very little more work required to achieve your goals. You will not be required to work more overtime, starve yourself, or learn the equivalent of a Master's degree in business administration. You will need some knowledge. You can acquire the knowledge you need in just a few hours, including the time spent in reading this book. Certainly, this task does not take too much hard work.

I want to be wealthy provided that I'm still young enough to enjoy it. Right now you're young compared to your age 20 or 30 or 40 years from now. So, this plan proposes that you spend a little less while you're definitely still young enough to enjoy it. The purpose is to hopefully have much more when you're older, less active, or maybe even dead! Wow! This looks like a tough one to reconcile.

Certainly, we all need recreation and we like to have fun at any age of life. At young ages, we have so many more options. We can climb mountains, sleep in a tent in the snow, kayak white water rivers, hike to the most remote and best places to hunt and fish, water ski on a single ski, and hike in the Grand Canyon to name a few. The good news is that with all these options, there are many which can be done inexpensively by young people. Additionally, many of these activities are even more fun if they are done inexpensively. For example, if you like to see the sights in our national parks, backpacking and camping is a much more fun way to do it than driving the roads and staying in hotels each night. What you'll see in the interior is so much better than what you generally see from the roads. Of course, the backpacking and camping option is also less expensive. The point is you can have more fun with less money when you're young. When you get older, you'll need more money to do similar things.

The next point is that in many activities the highest levels of satisfaction require more money than a young person has. Consequently, he or she must save and invest a small portion of income to reach the highest levels at a later time in life. For example, some of the best fishing in the world is in Alaska and Russia. Much of the best art is in Europe. A good savings and investment program could provide enough funds to make not just one trip but many trips to far away destinations.

Today, health professionals believe that most young people can have excellent health and stamina well into their senior years. The phrase, "in all things practice moderation," has more merit now than ever before because modern medicine, nutrition, and exercise enable us to have a high quality of life for a good many years after normal retirement age. It's even entirely feasible to acquire the funds needed for your ultimate experiences well before retirement. For example, sailors who begin early enough, could acquire the funds needed to purchase a luxury yacht by age 55. Without a good investment program, most young sailors would never be able to do it.

What are the ultimate experiences in your favorite hobbies? At what ages do you need the required funds? How much money would you need at today's prices? I mention experiences and hobbies in the plural to encourage you to think of several, rather than just one. Take the yacht example above. You want the yacht by age 55 because at 55 you'd be able to enjoy your yacht for 10 or 15 or 20 years or more. If you had to wait until, say age 70, you believe you'd be too old to enjoy sailing the yacht very much. So you want it by age 55. How much money does the yacht cost? Right now, a yacht like the one you want costs, say, $250,000. Of course, that particular yacht may cost significantly more by the time you're 55. You'll have to estimate the future rate of annual price inflation to calculate approximately how much money you'll need at age 55. The other items of information you'll need to make your calculations are your current age and the expected rate of return on your investments. The needed formulas and explanations are provided in Appendix B. Take the time now to make your list of ultimate experiences. For now, list what you want and how much it costs today. Do this for each of your hobbies.

My ultimate experiences:

1.

2.

3.

4.

Practicing moderation is more easily said than done. Most people will be excessive in spending and have very little money to set aside for the future. Some other people will be so fearful of poverty in old age that they save excessively and thereby miss good opportunities now. So what's the moderate or correct amount to save? There's no "one size fits all" answer to that question. If you want to accumulate $1 million and you're young enough, you should be able to do it by following the guidelines in this book. Some of you will not want to accumulate $1 million or have enough time to do it. However, you can realistically expect to enjoy substantial future benefits by following the guidelines in this book. You'll have fun and recreation while achieving your goals. Furthermore, using the right techniques, you'll hardly notice that some of your current earnings are being set aside for your future experiences.

I want to be wealthy provided that people remain more important to me than money. This "provided that" seems to be a rational reason for avoiding wealth. However, it is based more on stereotype and emotion than on reason. We've all seen wealthy people on television and movies. We've all read about them in newspapers and magazines. Perhaps we even personally know a very wealthy person. It's easy to stereotype wealthy people and assume that all wealthy people have the same negative personality traits. Some wealthy industrialists seem to care more about money than people. Their workers toil in sweatshops in order to make them rich. They become snobbish and insensitive. Some become celebrities and can't go anywhere without the press and photographers watching their every move.

Honestly ask yourself: does it have to be that way for wealthy people? Are there wealthy people who are not like that? Of course there are many. There are numerous wealthy people who care more about people than money, as evidenced by their donations of time and money to charities. Most provide their workers with decent wages and working conditions. They are not all snobbish and insensitive, and most are not celebrities. Don't let an emotional reaction against one or two wealthy people cause you to believe they are all that way. You can be the same person with $1 million as you are without it. Actually, you'll probably be a little nicer to other people than you are now. You won't have to be in such a rush to make ends meet. You can slow down and spend a little more time with your friends and family because you won't be so worried about money.

I want to be wealthy provided that my relatives don't hound me to death for "loans"; provided that my friends don't become envious of me and withdraw their friendship. Although most of us would like to have some control over other people, we don't really control anyone but ourselves. You can't control whether or not relatives ask for handouts or friends leave you. Maybe they will; maybe they won't. You don't really know. However, if they do change their behavior because of your wealth, it will be 25 or more years from now. It takes that long to accumulate wealth following the principles of this book. So cross that bridge when you come to it. Nobody except you needs to know how much money you have. In fact, most millionaires live modestly, and their neighbors have no idea how wealthy they are. As far as friends are concerned, your real friends will stick with you even if they know you have more money than they do. Some envious acquaintances may not stick with you, but then they weren't real friends anyway. In any case, you'll be able to travel, meet new people, and make new friends. You can have some friends with little money and other friends with a lot of money. So don't worry about what some other people might think 25 years or so from now!

I want to be wealthy provided nobody is harmed by my success. Some methods of wealth accumulation do indeed harm others. Some people have become very rich by working in the business of illegal drugs. Some perfectly legal corporations provide unsafe working conditions which cause their production workers to develop cancer or to die in accidents. In some communities, all of the wealthy people have achieved their wealth from one of the above described activities. However, even if you live in one of these communities, you can acquire wealth without exploiting other people. You may not have good role models to guide you, but you can do it. You can then be a good role model to others. By following the principles in this book you can achieve your goals, accumulate wealth, and become respected in your community. You can accomplish these objectives without harming or exploiting others. This book shows you how to do it.

Your success in becoming wealthy will actually help other people. Your savings and investments indirectly enable businesses to acquire capital goods, such as factories and equipment. Those capital goods will create jobs, products, and services which benefit the entire economy.

I want to be wealthy provided it doesn't take too much time from my family. You enjoy your family and like to spend time with them. Perhaps the pay scale in your occupation is limited, but you enjoy your work and you have time for your family. For you, wealth creation is not now a major goal and will never be something to devote much time to. This book is for you! You can have an enjoyable career, time with your family, and accumulate wealth at the same time.

I want to be wealthy provided that it doesn't spoil my children. Realize that this is a long term program. Your children will have graduated from high school by the time this program works for you. So it won't spoil your children. It may greatly help your children if you start the program as soon as they are born. You could be in a position to pay some, most, or all of their post high school education expenses if you so desire. The general principles of this book will show you how you can accumulate funds for any goal.

I want to be wealthy provided that the mundane aspects of money management don't stifle my creativity. "I don't have the patience to create a monthly budget and then keep track of every penny I spend. I'm not interested in reading *The Wall Street Journal* every day. I don't have the financial background to do good money management, and I'm not going to stifle my creativity to get it. Money matters are for people who get college degrees in business administration. Money management is really boring when you get down to it."

If that's your attitude, this book is for you! You don't have to track every penny you spend or read "The Wall Street Journal." You don't have to think about money day after day. Actually, you'll probably think and worry about money much less if you follow the simple guidelines in this book.

You're doing creative work and making a real contribution to society. You enjoy your work; it's fulfilling to you. Yet you do worry from time to time that you may not have money to help pay college tuition for your children. You may be concerned about financial needs of your aging parents. Perhaps, you have other financial goals that cannot usually be attained in your career, on your salary. So, chances are you already do think about money. If not, you probably will in a few years.

By utilizing the guidelines of this book, you'll actually be able to think about money less because you'll have fewer money worries. Instead of having to compromise your creativity, you'll actually enhance it by using the guidelines in this book.

I want to be wealthy provided that I can still be my own person. If you feel that your parents neglected you because they put too much emphasis on money, you may subconsciously avoid wealth. You want to do things differently than your parents did. Nevertheless, just because you feel that your parents put too much emphasis on money doesn't mean that wealth is bad. It doesn't mean that avoiding wealth is a good decision for you. It's not the quantity of money that's the problem here. It's the priorities. You can be your own person and have even more money than your parents. You can have money as well as time for your children and other activities. With a more balanced perspective, money can be seen as an opportunity to provide comforts and services to family members, others, and to yourself. Money can be seen as a way to have more security and independence. In short, you can value money not for itself, but as a means to accomplish other important, personal priorities.

I want to be wealthy provided that it doesn't change my spirituality. Wealth and spirituality are not contradictory. Nothing in any of the world's great religions teaches that wealthy people are evil or that wealthy people cannot be spiritual people.

CHAPTER 3

THE BEST BARGAIN IN TOWN

This is an opportunity you can't afford to miss. Do you like a bargain? Hard to believe, but Uncle Sam offers the best one going. If you're lucky, your employer is offering you a raise to take that bargain!

If you qualify, the federal government will allow you to reduce your taxable income and thereby reduce your current federal income taxes. So, what do you have to do to get this income tax deduction? You have to pay yourself first in the form of a contribution to a tax-sheltered retirement account. You win both ways! You get lower taxes now, and you fund your long-term goals.

An Avalanche of Money

Outstanding growth is achieved through the combination of tax deferral and compounding. Compounding in this context is interest earned on previously earned interest or gains earned on previously earned gains.

The growth is like a pebble dropped from a rocky mountain top causing a mountain slide or an avalanche. At the beginning, it doesn't look like much. One pebble hits another one or two small pebbles. They hit several more pebbles which in turn dislodge a small rock. The small rock hits another small rock and those two small rocks cause a larger rock to start rolling. The process accelerates until many large boulders come crashing down the mountainside.

The compounded growth of your savings account starts off small like the single pebble. Gradually and slowly at first, it increases in

24

size. The first two or three years produce results so small that you may say why bother, why keep going with it. Those with the wisdom and fortitude to continue can expect to see good results in five or ten years. Setting aside $1000 per year at 12% compounded growth produces $19,655 after ten years. Most people have never had that much money. For some it is too tempting to take that money now and enjoy it. We all need a new car, a bigger vacation, or whatever. We've worked hard. We've earned it and we deserve to spend it. But if we do, we get the small rocks and miss out on the huge boulders. In the second ten-year period, the account grows from $19,655 to $80,699. Now, we're getting a really good rock slide. If you're young enough to keep with this program and it continues to grow an average of 12% annually, you'll have $608,835 in 37 years. Now we're talking about an avalanche of big boulders. Big money. $1000 per year is only $83.33 a month. Double that investment to $2000 per year and the end result is $1,217,671! It's no wonder that the great scientist Albert Einstein called compound interest "the most powerful force in the universe." Figure 3-1 shows in graphic form the dramatic effect of time on investment results.

Figure 3-1
$2000 per year growing at 12% compounded annually

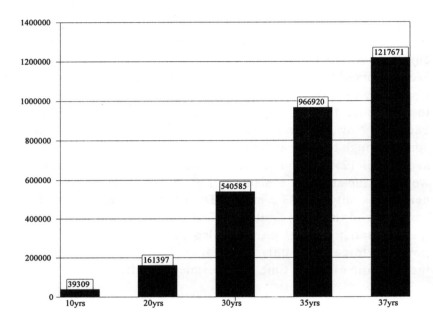

There are three factors which determine how much your account will compound or grow. They are:

1. The amount you can invest.
2. The rate of return, which is the expected annual percentage increase in value. It includes interest, dividends, capital gains, and capital appreciation. The rate of return is strongly affected by two factors: the level of risk and whether or not income is taxed currently.
3. The timing of your investment.

Obviously, the results are directly related to the amount of money you can invest. The relationship is one to one. That is, if you invest $2000 per year, the ending total will be twice the ending total from a $1000 per year contribution. Three thousand dollars per year will produce three times the ending result of $1000 per year and so on.

With the other two factors, the results are not one to one. Figure 3-2 shows the ending results of $2,000 per year for 37 years at three rates of compounded growth. Notice that the difference in ending values between 6% and 12% is far more than double.

Figure 3-2
Growth of $2000 per year for 37 years at various rates of increases

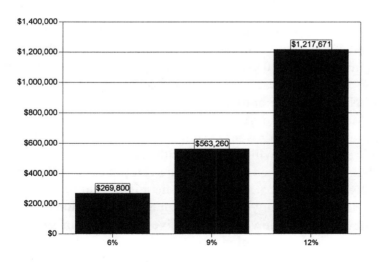

Generally speaking, higher rates of return are associated with higher risk. In Chapter 9, we'll discuss the risk/return relationship.

Tax deferral of investment gains is critical to achieving outstanding long-term results. But why does tax deferral produce better results? With tax deferral, you're earning income on money that would have already been paid to the government as taxes. That makes a huge difference over a long period of time.

Assume a 12% before-tax return reduced to a 9% return after a hypothetical 25% tax rate. Per the previous example in Figure 3-2, the result at 9% is $563,260. With tax deferral, the ending after-tax value is $913,253 ($1,217,671 - $304,418 in taxes). Thus, income tax deferral increases the after-tax result from $563,260 to $913,253.

Long time equals big money

The longer you leave your money invested, the better your results will be. Once again, the relationship is not one to one. It is like an avalanche. Most of the growth occurs in the last few years. So it is critical to start as young as possible and leave your money invested as long as you can reasonably do so. The temptation for some young people is to say, "I'm not making much money right now. Instead of investing $2000 per year now, I' ll wait until my 40s and invest, say, $4000 per year then. That will make up the difference, won't it?" No, it won't, not by a long shot.

Meet Martha and George. Martha knows it's important to start early but she really doesn't want to think that she has to save money for her entire life. She's willing to live with roommates for now and she's willing to drive a used car so that she can put away $2000 per year for 12 years. After that, she figures she might want to spend all she makes and not save any more. George on the other hand wants to drive new cars and have an expensive apartment in order to impress his girl friends. He plans to start his savings plan when he turns 46 years old. He'll invest $4000 per year. He'll do so until age 60. So Martha invests $2000 annually for 12 years beginning at age 23, while George invests $4000 annually for 15 years. They both leave the money invested until age 60. Table 3-1 shows how well each of them did, assuming 12% annual compounded growth.

Table 3-1

Martha's Early Start vs. George's Late Start					
	Martha			George	
Age	Annual	Year-end	Age	Annual	Year-end
23	$2,000	$2,240			
24	2,000	4,748			
25	2,000	7,558			
26	2,000	10,704			
27	2,000	14,230			
28	2,000	18,178			
29	2,000	22,598			
30	2,000	27,550			
31	2,000	33,096			
32	2,000	39,308			
33	2,000	46,266			
34	2,000	54,058			
35		60,545			
40		106,700			
46		210,606	46	$4,000	$4,480
47		235,879	47	4,000	9,496
48		264,184	48	4,000	15,116
49		295,886	49	4,000	21,412
50		331,392	50	4,000	28,460
51		371,159	51	4,000	36,356
52		415,698	52	4,000	45,200
53		465,582	53	4,000	55,104
54		521,452	54	4,000	66,196
55		584,026	55	4,000	78,620
56		654,109	56	4,000	92,532
57		732,602	57	4,000	108,226
58		820,515	58	4,000	125,572
59		918,976	59	4,000	145,120
60		$1,029,253	60	4,000	$167,012
Total	$24,000			$60,000	

George started late and invested $60,000 which grew to $167,012. Martha started early, investing only $24,000 which grew to $1,029,253! Time is money. The longer the better.

All three factors played a major role in producing outstanding results for Martha. $2000 per year in savings is not easy for most young people. Resisting the temptation to spend any of those funds from age 34 to age 60 is also difficult. A twelve percent annualized rate of return is excellent by most standards. It's also been quite attainable historically with investments in the stock market and mutual funds which own common stocks.

Tax-deferred retirement accounts

Tax accountants and corporate benefits specialists have their own classifications for retirement plans. From your standpoint, tax-deferred retirement plans can be divided into three groups. The first segment is the Individual Retirement Account (IRA), which is available independently of your employer. The second group is employer-sponsored plans which allow the employee to make contributions to his or her own retirement account. The employer can also make contributions to these accounts. This group includes 401(k) plans. It also includes some employer-sponsored IRA plans. The third group is employer-sponsored plans totally controlled by the employer and funded only by the employer. These include pension plans and profit sharing plans. Your employer may have both types of employer-sponsored plans, just one of them, or no plan at all.

Since the purpose of this book is to help you, an employee, make savings and investment decisions, we will not cover plans totally controlled by the employer. If you are self-employed, you may want to look into information about Keogh plans, which are not covered here. Keogh plans have many similarities to 401(k) plans. Another popular plan not covered in this book is the Tax-Sheltered Annuity (TSA) authorized by Internal Revenue Code Section 403(b). The TSA is offered to its employees by charitable, tax-exempt organizations such as churches and schools. The TSA is also very similar to the 401(k) salary reduction plan.

In this book, we'll focus on the two most popular tax-deferred plans: the IRA and the 401(k). 401(k) plans are sometimes called thrift plans, tax-deferred savings plans, or salary reduction plans. If your employer sponsors a plan which is not a 401(k), read about these two plans anyway. The background you'll get here will be very beneficial to you in your evaluation of your employer's plan.

Ask your supervisor to see if your employer offers a tax-deferred savings plan that you can make contributions to. If a plan does exist, ask for a copy of the benefits book to see if you are eligible to participate. Most employees are. Most large employers offer one of these plans. Many small employers do not offer any savings plan. If your employer offers any of these plans, the employer will automatically offer the plan to you when you first become eligible to participate.

Generally speaking, if you make a withdrawal from any tax-deferred plan prior to age 59½, you will owe an additional 10% penalty tax on the distribution. There are several important exceptions. New rules allow IRA withdrawals for purchase of home or higher education, penalty tax free. For more information about withdrawals and related tax considerations, you can ask your employee benefits representative or provider of your IRA. Don't make any withdrawals without reviewing the current tax rules first.

A modest withdrawal can substantially reduce the ending value of your account. For example, let's make the assumption that you're contributing $2000 per year and earning 12% compounded growth. At the end of year seven, your account value is $22,599. You've worked hard for this money, and now you decide to take $10,000 out to pay for your daughter's wedding, a new car, a fishing boat or something else that's important. Assuming continued contributions and growth in the account, the ending value of the account in 37 years is $918,071. If the withdrawal had not been made, the account would be worth $1,217,671. Thus, $10,000 now cost $299,600 later!

Some 401(k) plans allow borrowing and some do not. Borrowing is far better than making a withdrawal. A withdrawal is subject to income tax. If you borrow from your 401(k), there is no penalty tax or income tax. Borrowing will most likely lower the total investment performance of your account, but not nearly as much as a withdrawal. With borrowing, your 401(k) account will gain the interest income you pay on the loan, but it will lose potential investment gains. Even though borrowing is much better than withdrawing, I recommend against borrowing except in real emergencies. The interest expense is not deductible on your tax return, assuming the loan is for consumer goods. The most important thing, the primary purpose of the plan, is to accumulate a substantial nest egg. To the extent that the interest rate you pay on the loan is less than the gains you could make in the account, the loan will significantly reduce the ending value of the account. It's far better to save in advance for both short term goals and long term goals.

The 401(k) Plan

The 401(k) plan is the only tax-deferred retirement account with a numeric name. The 401 number is the Internal Revenue Code section which deals with tax-deferred savings plans of all sorts. Paragraph k under Section 401 describes this particular type of plan.

Basically, the 401(k) plan is an arrangement set up by your employer which allows you to contribute to your own tax-deferred retirement account. Your contribution is handled by payroll deduction. The employer has an option of making matching contributions into your account. There is a limit on the amount of contributions you can make, and the limit changes each year. As of 1998 the limit is $10,000. Your payroll deduction contributions are always 100% vested. That is they belong to you no matter what. Depending on the company's rules, some or all of your company's contributions to your account are forfeited if you leave the company within a stated number of years. The longest permitted requirement of 100% vesting is seven years. Many companies have shorter requirements for full vesting. The Summary Plan Description explains all this and provides the company's vesting schedule.

The intent of the plan is that the money will be taken out as a lump sum or as a series of payments after age 59½. A 10% penalty tax generally applies on withdrawals prior to age 59½. You may be able to borrow money from your plan without the penalty tax and you may be able to withdraw money for a hardship. If you leave your employer, you can roll over the entire amount into an IRA in order to keep the benefits of tax deferred compound growth. For more details about your company's 401(k) plan, read the information provided by your employee-benefits representative.

Investment options

If your company has a 401(k) plan, it is most probably, but not necessarily, an outstanding opportunity for you. In your initial evaluation, look first at the types of investment options available to you. If your contributions must go into a piece of land, commodities, or collectibles, then avoid the 401(k) plan. It might produce an excellent return, but the risk of loss is too great for most people. Instead of this 401(k), put your money into an IRA. Some employers offer a wide variety of investment options for both employer contributions and employee contributions. Generally, these plans are excellent. Some other employers restrict investment options to the company stock, as explained below. Chapter 7 will provide more detailed information about appropriate investments for your 401(k) and IRA.

Company matching contributions

Next, find out whether your employer matches your contribution with a company contribution. If so, how much or what percentage of your contribution is matched? Many companies provide a match of 50 cents or more on each dollar of employee contribution. A match of 50 cents or a dollar for each employee dollar can make a 401(k) plan extremely attractive. In effect, a 50% matching contribution is a 50% gain on your investment! Additionally in this example, 150% of your out-of-pocket investment will be earning future income.

Company stock in the 401(k) plan

Some employers offer investment options for employee contributions but make their matching contributions only in the employer's stock. Some other employers offer no investment options; all employer and employee contributions go into company stock only. Are these plans good for the employees? Let's consider each type. In the first example, the employer makes matching contributions with employer stock. The employees' contributions can go into other investments such as mutual funds. The general rule is that diversification is the most effective way to reduce risk. Diversification and risk are more fully explained in Chapter 9. Briefly, a well-diversified portfolio has no more than 5% of assets in a single investment. If the employer match is one dollar for each employee dollar, then 50% of the combined portfolio will be in one investment. If the employer match is 50 cents to the employee's dollar, then ⅓ of the total portfolio is in a single investment. According to investment theory, such portfolios (50% or 33% in one stock) are extremely risky. However, in the real world, these portfolios can have low risk if the employees' contributions are well diversified. Remember that it's the employer's contributions, not money out of your pocket, going into the company stock. If the employer goes bankrupt, you lose none of your own contributions, and you can get excellent results on your own contributions. If the company stock does well, then your total results can be outstanding.

In the other type of plan described above, where both employer and employee contributions must go into company stock, the risks are greater. The rewards can also be greater. Many employees put their own contributions into company stock even in those plans which have other options. In many cases, the results are outstanding. In some other cases, the employer goes bankrupt, and all of the employees' money is lost.

In this type of plan, you first want to evaluate the risk of your employer going bankrupt. See if the company is rated by *Standard & Poor's* or *Moody's*. Standard & Poor's and Moody's are companies which evaluate bond investments. Most libraries have one or both of these services. If the company has corporate bonds which are rated A or better, it is not at high risk for bankruptcy (see Chapter 7 for more information on bond ratings). If the employer doesn't have bonds rated by S&P or Moody's, then your evaluation process will be more difficult. If the employer has a high debt load or low earnings, it's probably too risky to participate in the 401(k) plan. In any case, it could be a good idea to have a professional, such as a CPA, look over the employer's financial statements and give you a professional opinion. This 401(k) plan will probably be very successful for you if all these conditions are met:

1. The company is in strong financial shape.
2. The company matches your contributions dollar for dollar.
3. You are fully vested or will probably become fully vested in the plan.

Even if the company's stock goes down somewhat, you can still come out a winner. For example, if the employer's match is dollar for dollar, the company stock could drop 50%, and the total value of the portfolio would equal your own contributions. In effect, the employer's contributions would be wiped out, but yours would be OK assuming you were fully vested. In this example, the stock would have to go down more than 50% for you to lose money in the plan. If the stock did not go up or down, your investment would increase 100% due to the employer's matching contribution.

In summary, the risk is greater in these company stock-only plans. Since the risk is high, be sure to carefully evaluate the plan before joining.

Don't you want a raise?

These 401(k) plans are often called salary reduction plans. Salary reduction sounds horrible. If your employer makes matching contributions, the 401(k) plan is really a salary enhancement plan or a salary increase plan.

Assuming the plan offers good investment options and assuming the employer matches your contributions, you can't afford to stay out of the plan. It's just too much of a bargain to miss out on. The employer's contribution is, in effect, an increase in pay for you. You do want an increase in pay, don't you? No additional hours of work or added responsibilities involved. When contributing to a 401(k) plan, your contributions and your employer's matching contributions are not subject to current federal income tax. Your current year income taxes decrease as a result of your contributions. You don't have to pay income taxes until the money is withdrawn from the account. Look at it this way; if you don't put money into your 401(k) plan, you'll have to pay federal and state income taxes on that money now. With the 401(k) and company matching contribution, your choice is this: do I want a raise or do I want to pay more income taxes now? Do I want to pay myself or do I want to pay the government now? It's your choice.

So why would you turn down a raise? Either you don't understand the plan or you think you can't afford to take the raise. This book should help you understand the plan. Additionally, your employer's benefits representative can help explain the 401(k) plan and give you printed information. If the plan is still too confusing, then seek advice from someone who is knowledgeable about these matters. The potential opportunity is too outstanding for you to miss due to some initial confusion about it.

Other than a lack of understanding, the other major reason to avoid the plan is a belief that you can't afford to make a contribution to it. When you ask yourself the question, "can I afford to make the 401(k) contribution," your quick answer is no. You believe that you don't have any money to pay yourself first. You're already living paycheck to paycheck. There's nothing to save. The more important question is this: "can I afford to turn down a pay raise (the employer's matching contribution)?" Chapters four and five will show you how you can afford to make the contribution and thereby get the matching pay increase.

Another objection to making 401(k) contributions is that the employee doesn't want to tie up the money for 20 to 40 years until retirement. To solve this problem, many employers offer the benefit of letting employees borrow from their 401(k) plans. When the employee pays off the loan, the interest expense goes into the 401(k) account, not to your friendly finance company.

Start small, but start now

Contribute what you can to the 401(k) plan. For many people, 6% of their pay seems too much to contribute. You certainly don't want to start off contributing too much and then have to quit the plan. So start small. If 6% is too much, then contribute 3%. When you get an increase in pay, put half of your increase into additional contributions so that over a period of time you increase your contributions to 6% of gross pay. That way you get both more take home money and more savings each time you get an increase in pay. In addition, the company's matching contribution will increase as your contribution increases. You'll get two raises: one regular pay increase and one a company paid savings contribution. If possible, continue increasing your contributions up to at least the percentage that your company matches. That percentage varies from one company to another. Not all are 6%.

Start your tax-deferred savings plan now, even if it's a small start. If you put off starting now, you'll just have the same or similar reasons for delay later. Starting small now is infinitely better than doing nothing now. Time can work magic for those who start now.

Certainly if you can afford to do so and if your plan is a good one, contribute up to the maximum amount allowed each year. You can't count on working your whole life for your current employer. You can't count on the government to keep the rules the same. At some future point in time, the government may substantially reduce the maximum contribution allowed. So make hay while the sun shines.

Additionally, you can't count on historical investment returns to continue indefinitely into the future. So, even if you've been getting 12% or more compounded growth the last few years, there is no guarantee you'll do that well in the future. So, it's a good idea to contribute more money each year to make up for potential decreases in future growth.

Employer administration of 401(k) plans

There have been some problems with 401(k) plan administration. Previously, the employer was allowed up to 90 days after payroll deduction to deposit the plan contributions. Ninety days was a long time for the employer to enjoy an interest free loan from its employees. As of Feb. 3, 1997, the U. S. Labor Department, which oversees the nation's 401(k) plans, changed the regulations. Now, employers must make these deposits by the 15th day of the month following the month in which the payroll deduction was made. That change is a substantial improvement in the regulations.

There have been a few cases of theft of 401(k) assets, and such problems are not covered by insurance. However, this should not cause alarm to 401(k) plan participants. The Labor Department has successfully recovered money for the plan participants in many, but not all, of those theft cases. According to the U. S. Labor Department's Pension and Welfare Benefits Administration, the vast majority of 401(k) plans are safe.

There are a few things you can do to check up on the administration of your 401(k) plan. You can compare the total contributions from your pay stubs to the total contributions on your 401(k) statements. If the figures aren't equal, ask your plan administrator or benefits representative to explain the difference. If you're still concerned, get a copy of your plan's "Summary Plan Description." By law you are entitled to a copy of this document, which lays out the rules your plan must follow. If you believe the plan is not following the rules, you can file a claim with the plan administrator and you can appeal the administrator's ruling. If you're still not satisfied, you can contact the Labor Department's Pension and Welfare Benefits Administration. The Labor Department gets involved if the number of employees is more than 100.

The IRA: Outstanding Even if Not Tax Deductible

The regular IRA is a plan which allows you to contribute up to $2000 per year to an investment account. You choose what types of investments you want in the plan. To set up the IRA, you can go to a bank, savings & loan, credit union, insurance company, stock broker, mutual fund, or trust company. One nice advantage of an IRA is that you have control over the contribution amount. Each year you can choose any amount to contribute, from zero up to $2000.

Almost anyone receiving "earned income" is eligible to contribute to an IRA. Earned income is earnings from employment. It includes wages, commissions, tips, fees, alimony, and all other amounts received for performing personal services. It does not include interest, dividends, capital gains. Spouses of workers with earned income are also allowed to contribute up to $2000, even if the spouse doesn't have earned income of his or her own.

The IRA is an outstanding opportunity whether or not it is tax deductible for you. Most people mistakenly believe that current income tax reduction on their IRA contribution is the most important benefit. The sales literature of banks, stock brokers, and mutual funds stress this benefit to create new IRAs. Indeed, professional tax return preparers often recommend IRAs only to those eligible to deduct IRA contributions. However, tax deferred compounded growth over the life of the account is by far the best feature of an IRA. For an example, see Table 3-2 on page 42.

Who is eligible to deduct IRA contributions?

Because the tax laws are so complex and change so frequently, taxpayers should get complete updated information on this and all other tax topics. The following rules relate to deducting IRA contributions for 1998 on the tax return due April 15, 1999. You can deduct the lesser of $2000 or 100% of your earned income if you meet any one of these conditions:

1. Neither you nor your spouse is a "covered participant" for any part of the year in an employer-sponsored tax deferred retirement plan.

2. You are not a "covered participant" in such a retirement plan but your spouse is a "covered participant." Your combined modified adjusted gross income is less than $150,000.

3. You are a "covered participant" but your adjusted gross income is less than the "income limit."

Your employee-benefits representative can tell you whether or not you are a "covered participant" under these rules. Even if your employer doesn't offer a 401(k) plan, you could still be covered in an employer-sponsored retirement plan if the employer has a pension plan. If you are a covered participant, depending on your income and filing status (single, married, etc.) you may deduct all, none, or some of your IRA contribution. Check the current income limits in your income tax return instructions; the limits change each year. You can have both an IRA and a 401(k). If you have both, you can make IRA contributions but you can't deduct the contributions on your tax return unless your income is below the current income limit.

New SIMPLE IRA and 401(k) plans

Beginning in 1996, there are two new options for companies with no more than 100 employees. They are the SIMPLE IRA and SIMPLE 401(k). The two options are practically identical. These plans allow an employee to contribute up to $6000 per year. Generally, the employer must match the employees' contributions up to 3% of employee compensation, or the employer has to make a 2% contribution to each employee's account. The employee can contribute any percentage of salary up to $6000. These plans offer outstanding new benefits to employer and employee. The major new benefit for employers is that the employer will be able to increase his or her own tax-deferred savings to $6000. The added expense of making contributions to employee accounts should be relatively small for most employers. Also, these plans truly are simple. They require no significant administrative expenses. Typically, the custodian charges each account a modest annual maintenance fee. The employees get the major new benefit of being able to save up to $6000 each year, rather than being limited to $2000 in their own IRA. Many mutual fund companies and insurance companies offer the SIMPLE plans. These plans should become extremely popular as more and more employers find out about the new law. The plan must be established between January 1 and October 1. I encourage all small employers (less than 100 employees) to get complete information on the SIMPLE IRA from one or two mutual fund companies.

The $1,000,000 nondeductible IRA

Ever since the IRA became nondeductible for many taxpayers, the financial press has generally downplayed the advantages of a nondeductible IRA. Partly, this is due to the fact that wealthy taxpayers can utilize tax-deferred annuities, without the contribution limit of $2000. It's also due to the fact that most of the tax benefits are well into the future, while many Americans only want to know what's in it for me right now. In terms of tax savings, there is no current benefit. The benefit is tax deferment of future earnings in the IRA. Consider the income deferral of a nondeductible IRA in Table 3-2.

Table 3-2
Income on IRAs is tax deferred
$2000 annual contribution at 12% compounded growth

Year	Out of pocket contribution	Account value at end of year
1	$2,000	$2,240
5	10,000	14,230
10	20,000	39,309
20	40,000	161,397
30	60,000	540,585
35	70,000	966,926
36	72,000	1,085,197
37	$74,000	$1,217,671

The investment gain in this example is the ending value of $1,217,671 less the total contributions of $74,000 or a net gain of $1,143,671. Therefore, this nondeductible IRA enjoys future tax deferral on $1,143,671 income. A fully deductible IRA would enjoy deferral on the full $1,217,671.

Since tax deferral on investment gains produces practically all of an IRA's benefits over a long period of years, a nondeductible IRA is almost as good as a deductible IRA for young people. So, if you can afford the $2000 per year, you should have your own IRA, deductible or not. Since your contributions are nondeductible, when you take money out of such an IRA, a portion of the proceeds is tax free. If you qualify for a Roth IRA, discussed later in this chapter, then fund a Roth IRA rather than a nondeductible regular IRA. All proceeds from a Roth IRA are tax free.

Moving from one IRA to another IRA

Once every 12 months you can roll over your current IRA into another IRA. While doing so, you can hold the money for up to 60 days before putting it into the new IRA. So, in effect, you can borrow the entire amount for up to 60 days each 12 months. However, if you do this more often than once each twelve months, you will be taxed as though you received a distribution and kept it.

An easier and better way to change your IRA is to make a trustee to trustee transfer. To do this, you request that your financial institution or mutual fund send the money directly to the other IRA trustee. You can do the trustee to trustee transfer as often as you like without incurring tax problems.

New Roth IRA

Generally speaking, if something sounds too good to be true, it probably is. A salesman is probably trying to sell you a bad deal. In the case of the Roth IRA, it sounds too good to be true; but it is true! In effect, within the Roth IRA, income taxes and capital gains taxes are reduced to zero if a few easy requirements are met. The Roth IRA, which is named after U.S. Senate Finance Chairman William V. Roth, Jr. (R-Del.), became available in 1998. The annual payments to the Roth IRA are limited to $2000 per year for a single taxpayer and $4000 for joint filers. Spouses of workers with earned income are allowed to contribute up to $2000 to a Roth IRA. The Roth IRA contributions are not tax deductible on your tax return. However, earnings in the Roth IRA are tax free under certain conditions. Yes **TAX FREE**, not just tax-deferred. Earnings are tax free if you keep the money in the account for at least five years and if you meet any of these other conditions.

1. The money is withdrawn on or after age 59½.
2. The money goes to a beneficiary or your estate after you die.
3. The money is withdrawn when you become disabled.
4. You withdraw the money (up to $10,000) to buy your first home.

The Roth IRA has other advantages over regular IRAs. Contributions (not earnings) can be withdrawn tax free at any time for any purpose. Additionally, the Roth IRA can continue to grow as long as the investor desires, as there is no age requirement for distributions to begin.

You can contribute to a Roth IRA even if you have a retirement plan at work. There are income limits on who can have a Roth IRA. When a single person's adjusted gross income reaches $95,000, the maximum contribution starts going down. By $110,000 it is totally phased out. With joint filers the phase out begins at $150,000 and is gone at $160,000.

Additionally, taxpayers with adjusted gross income of less than $100,000 can convert their regular IRA to Roth IRAs beginning in 1998. Converting requires that income taxes be paid on the entire IRA (less nondeductible contributions, if any) during the year of conversion. The decision to convert or not to convert depends on a taxpayer's unique situation. Many older taxpayers within ten years of retirement who expect to be in a lower tax bracket after retirement may be better off not to convert to the Roth IRA. Most young taxpayers (more than ten years to retirement) with regular IRAs will benefit by converting, if they have the money outside the IRA to pay the taxes. The benefits of converting are lost if the tax money is taken from the IRA or other tax-deferred account. Young taxpayers will get higher after tax results by converting to the Roth IRA even if their tax rates are moderately lower in retirement. Additionally, young taxpayers will be better off to annually fund a Roth IRA rather than a regular IRA. Investors can easily get individualized advice on whether or not to utilize the Roth IRA. Several brokerage firms and mutual fund companies have developed computer software to help make these calculations. Free help is also available on the Internet from many sources, including brokerage firms and mutual fund companies. One such site is **www.strong-funds.com**. Most of these sites, including the one just mentioned, also have the current tax rules and other information about IRA, 401(k), and other retirement plans.

IRA or 401(k)?

Sometimes the best strategy is to have an IRA and avoid the 401(k) at work. In other situations, just the opposite would be appropriate. And for many people, having both makes the most sense. The flow chart on page 46 summarizes the following analysis.

First of all, determine whether or not the investment options in your 401(k) plan are good choices. If all choices are bad, the plan has too much risk. In that case, avoid the 401(k). It doesn't matter whether the company matches your contribution and allows you to borrow from your plan. If the investment options are all highly speculative, you could lose most or all of your money. You'd be better off in your own IRA. Most mutual funds which are invested in diversified portfolios of common stocks and/or bonds are good investment choices for your 401(k).

Second, determine whether the company makes matching contributions into your 401(k). If it does, you're generally better off in the 401(k) plan than your own IRA. Invest up to the maximum percentage that the employer matches. If you have more to invest than that amount and if you're not near retirement age, then fund a Roth IRA with the next $2000 of available savings. If you still have more money to invest, then continue to fund the 401(k) up to the maximum allowable by your employer.

If the employer does not offer matching contributions, then you need to determine whether or not you'll likely need to borrow money from your 401(k) plan sometime before retirement. Many corporations allow employees to borrow from their 401(k) plans, but you can't borrow from your IRA. If you want to borrow from your retirement account, then fund a 401(k) plan first. If you have more to invest than the maximum allowable in a 401(k), then fund your IRA next. If you don't plan to borrow from your retirement account and if there's no employer match, then you may be better off with your own IRA first. The reason is that with your own IRA you have an almost unlimited number of investment options. You can research the best investments. You're not limited to the choices in your employer's plan. Furthermore, the Roth IRA is usually better than

401(k) contributions which are not matched by the employer. It's better for young employees because the proceeds are tax free, as stated earlier. It's hard to write out a check each month; so get your IRA provider to automatically draft your checking account for your contributions.

Flow chart to choose 401(k), IRA, or both.
Figure 3-3

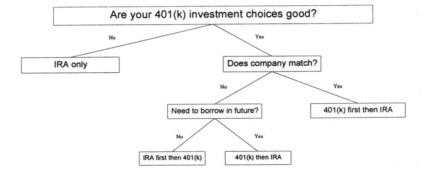

Distribution Options

If you're in a 401(k) plan and leave your employer prior to taking distributions from the plan, you have several options. The first option is to leave the account invested with the ex-employer. If you like the investment options in that plan, check with the employee benefits department to see what their rules are regarding leaving your account there. The company may have some restrictions on what you can do with your account.

The second option is to move your money into another tax-deferred investment account. You can roll over into a new employer's 401(k) or into an IRA. In all of the above options, you can maintain the tax-deferred status of your investments. The third option is to take your money out and pay income taxes.

There are several options or formulas for getting the money out of your 401(k) or IRA. Be sure to consult the current applicable rules before beginning your withdrawals. Generally speaking, you are required to start taking distributions by age 70½. The exception is Roth IRAs which don't have that requirement. There could be tax penalties for taking out too much or too little money each year. Also, there may be significant tax differences in taking a lump sum distribution vs. payments in installments. These rules change from time to time. Prior to retirement, it would be a good idea to consult with a tax or financial planner to help you choose the best distribution option for your circumstances. The counselor could also help you with the proper investment of your funds during your retirement years. Balance and diversification are important here. Even in your retirement years, some of your funds (but not all) should be invested in growth securities in order to hedge against inflation.

Tax-Deferred Insurance Products

Tax-deferred retirement plans are not the only investments providing income tax deferral. Whole life insurance and annuities also provide income tax deferral. The whole life or universal life policy is a combination of term insurance plus a tax-deferred investment. The term insurance component is life insurance which expires at the end of a year or at the end of several years. At the end of the term insurance policy, there is no cash value. The tax-deferred investment component of whole life insurance provides a buildup of cash values in the policy. An annuity policy is mostly a tax-deferred investment with a very small life insurance component. The insurance component is that if your investment loses money and you die before it goes back up to the break-even point, your heirs will get the original investment. It's not much insurance and it's rarely applied in practice. Most young people with modest incomes do not need whole life insurance. A term life insurance policy is generally all they need. For these young people who have enough money to buy whole life insurance, my advice is to get term insurance instead and invest the difference in an IRA or 401(k). Due to the higher average expenses of whole life and annuity products, you'll likely get better investment gains in a mutual fund than in the insurance products. After ten or twenty years of investing in an IRA or 401(k), your retirement account may be large enough that you can reduce or even eliminate your life insurance, depending on your family situation. If you have estate planning needs, then consider whole life insurance. However, most young people do not have estate planning needs.

If your income is more than enough to take full advantage of your IRA and/or 401(k), then consider annuities. However, don't put an annuity policy into your IRA. The annuity policy fees drag down the performance of the IRA. Instead you can find mutual funds with similar investment objectives and policies to put into your IRA.

CHAPTER 4

PAY YOURSELF FIRST

Earning More Money is Not the Answer.

Paying yourself first is essential if you are ever going to have any significant amount of savings. Pay yourself first, not last. That's the key.

Right now, you may be living from paycheck to paycheck. There's nothing to pay yourself. A logical conclusion is to cut back on certain expenses, which will free up some money at the end of the month. You can then pay yourself last – at the end of the month after everything else is paid. The problem is that even if you were able to accomplish that result and build up some money in your checking account, that money would soon disappear. Within a few weeks or months or a year that savings would be gone. It would somehow get spent on something else. It seems to be a law of human nature. We spend all that we earn.

If we are currently making $10,000, we spend all of it and think that we will start saving when our income goes to $20,000. If we're making $70,000, we spend all of it and think that we'll start saving when our income hits $100,000. And on it goes. The time to start is not later when our incomes increase. It's so easy to believe that working overtime or getting a second job will solve your money problems. Chances are your bills will increase with the additional work. You'll probably have to spend more money for transportation, clothes, and food. With more work and longer hours, you'll need even more rest and relaxation. In order to deal with the increased stress of extra work, you might spend more money on amusements and snacks.

You can't wait until your children have graduated from school. There's not enough time left at that point to produce substantial results. You can't even wait until all the bills are fully paid off to start a savings program. If bills are a problem now, they will always be a problem – until you start saving. Whatever your situation in life is, the time to start a savings program is now.

The key to making ends meet is the same as the key to accumulating $1,000,000. It is not making more money. It's the wise management of the money you are currently earning.

It's All About Choices.

As you'll see in the next chapter, little weekly savings can add up to hundreds of thousands of dollars over the years. So, every time you think about buying an ice cream desert or going to the movies, you either have to deny yourself, or feel guilty about doing it. Right? No, not at all. You pay yourself first, as soon as you get your paycheck. Pay yourself a modest amount and leave some funds available for fun. You'll then make choices about what recreation or amusements you want the most. There will be no guilt because you've already set aside something for your most important goals.

Paying yourself first is all about choices. It's not about sacrificing or missing out on some fun. It's about your choice in how you want to spend your money and what you want to spend it on. It's not about doing without. It's about doing with – all your goals and dreams, including the big expensive ones.

Of course, most of us know that we "should" be paying for this year's vacation this year, rather than next year. We "should" be saving for our children's college education, our own retirement, financial independence, etc.; and we will as soon as we have more money or fewer bills to pay.

Bills. What a depressing word that is. It's almost like punishment, but paying the bills is something we have to do. For most of us, the current goal is only to get the credit cards and loans paid off in addition to the never ending bills. Saving money will come after we get rid of the bills. It's a trap that most of us fall into. We concentrate on the short-term goal while ignoring the long-term.

Ignoring the long-term goals takes some fun out of your life. There's anticipation, hope, and joy in taking those necessary steps to accomplishing long-term goals. What are those big things you want? Think about actually doing those things. Taste it; feel it; imagine it. Plan for it to happen and then follow your plan!

Work on all your goals starting this month. You don't have to fully complete your shorter-range goals before working toward the longer-term. In fact, if you try to do that, you'll invariably wait too long. Paying yourself first is about accomplishing all your goals, not just today's goals. It's about making the choice to fulfill your highest financial dreams. It's about taking control of your life, rather than letting your bills and your amusements have control.

Every month we pay rent or mortgage, utility bills, gasoline, food, etc. But we don't pay the most important person – ourselves. If we pay ourselves anything at all, it's at the end of the year when we make a contribution to an Individual Retirement Account (IRA), if we have any money then. We usually don't. It's far better and obviously more successful to pay yourself first each month. Each time you get a paycheck, figure you owe yourself part of that amount. Put that portion in savings and then pay your bills.

The key elements in paying yourself first are to do it systematically and do it periodically, without fail. Do it at least once a month.

Dr. Stephen Covey has written a couple of outstanding books which relate very well to the importance of paying yourself first. The books are *The Seven Habits of Highly Effective People* and *First Things First*. One point I got from these books is that people generally spend an inordinate amount of time fighting fires rather than preventing fires from happening, so to speak. People spend an inordinate amount of time doing urgent "busy work" in comparison to time spent in achieving long-term goals. What brings meaning to our lives is doing the really important things. Dr. Covey says identify your values and goals and then do those things first. Don't wait until the lesser things are finished. Do the important things first. Otherwise, you'll never get around to doing them.

If you've never lived the life of a millionaire, it's hard to believe that you can become one. For most of us, it's easy to believe that we'll have a little less than our parents or about the same as our parents, if we work hard. If our parents are not millionaires, it's very difficult to believe that we can be millionaires. We may want some of the things that rich people have, but it's hard for us to imagine that we'll ever have them. We tend to stifle those dreams and desires because we believe they are impossible for us.

Since we don't think there's a chance of reaching our highest material goals, we tend to fritter away our money in an attempt to bring some momentary fun into our lives. Since we believe there never will be money for the "big things," we indulge ourselves in numerous small things like snacks, amusements, etc. If there's a few dollars available, better spend it now to have a little fun. Otherwise, it'll be gone to pay bills. So, we spend it and there's nothing left to put into savings.

In the financial realm, what's important is to accomplish your big goals: financial independence, a lakeside cottage, vacations to foreign countries, or whatever you want. Work toward those goals first. Pay yourself first. Then pay the other bills.

You Can Start Small

Saving money seems hard, but it doesn't have to be. In fact, it can be easy. For short-term goals, many people use the following method with great success. At the end of each day, put all your coins into a big jar. Earmark the jar for a specific goal. Periodically, put the coins into rolls. After the jar is full or after a certain amount of time has passed (anywhere from two weeks to a year), use the money from the jar to accomplish your goal.

You're now practicing the principle of delayed gratification. You could use the coins each day to buy yourself another cup of coffee or soda. Instead of getting that little gratification now, you're waiting for the jar to provide a much larger benefit to you later. It may sound silly, but it works.

The same basic principles apply to long-term goals. You don't have to start big. But you do have to start NOW.

All or nothing. It's certainly a great rationalization for procrastinating. Your long-term goals may cost so much money that it seems impossible to accomplish those goals with the little bit you can save now. You may think that if you can't put $100 per month into savings, why bother. It takes big bucks to pay for your financial dreams. You may think that any amount less than $100 per month, you might as well spend at a nice restaurant.

Yet, small amounts add up. $50 per month at 12% compounded annually grows to $154,212 in 30 years. No, that's not a million dollars, but it's a start. It's OK to start small. It's actually a good idea. After just a few months, you'll feel very good about your successful beginning. That success will motivate you to do more. Your motivation will gather momentum. After several months have passed, you'll probably find ways to increase your savings. In the meantime, you'll enjoy great satisfaction in working toward your goals. It's so important to just get started. Even if it's a small amount, it's a BIG step. You'll have the satisfaction of knowing that you are in control of your financial future.

Shouldn't I Pay Off Debts First?

Many financial planners maintain that the best strategy is to pay off high interest debts before starting a savings and investment plan. If the debt expense is higher than the rate of return on your investments, that strategy is logically correct. If your debt expense is 18% and your investments earn 10%, then from a strictly financial standpoint, you'd be 8% worse off by putting the money into investments as opposed to reducing the debt. Yet, I'm proposing that you do just that – partially. I say partially because I recommend some cash go to reducing debt and some go into your long-term investment account. If your employer does not have a matching

401(k) plan, most, but not all, of your available cash should go to reducing high interest debt. If your company does have a good, matching 401(k) plan, then try to save enough money to contribute the maximum amount your company will match plus enough to gradually pay down your debts. From an emotional standpoint, paying the debt is almost like a punishment. It's today's money paying for something old and past. Investing in the long-term account is quite the opposite emotionally. It's paying for something that you can't afford now but will hopefully have in the future. It's a reward rather than a punishment.

If you focus only on the debt, you miss out on the hope and anticipation of rewards in the investment account. If and when you finally do pay off all the debt, you're likely to celebrate by splurging too much; and that can put you right back into debt. From an emotional standpoint, it's best to work on all your goals at the same time. For most people, it's the only way that works.

Generally, the percentage of interest expense on personal debt exceeds the earnings rate on your investments. However, if you have a loan which has an interest expense less than the rate of return on your investments, then the recommended strategy is to pay no more on the loan than the minimum required each month. In other words, don't pay off the loan early. Investors with some low interest student loans may fit in this category. In any case, work on reducing debt and building your IRA or 401(k) investments at the same time.

Hide Your Long-Term Savings From Yourself

When you pay yourself first, you'll want to do it in such a way that you "hide" the money from yourself. Ideally, you don't want to have the money even for a second before it goes into your long-term investment account. If possible, use payroll deduction at your work. That way, you won't be tempted to spend the money before you are able to make the deposit yourself.

Payroll deduction is painless. You don't write a check; you don't even see the money. It's deducted from your paycheck and goes straight into your savings account. Since you don't see that money to begin with, you don't miss it. If you don't bring it home, you won't have the great urge it spend it. In most cases, the best payroll deduction plan for long-term goals is the 401(k) plan where you work. Otherwise, use payroll deduction or automatic draft from your checking account to make contributions to your individual retirement account (IRA).

It is important to view these payroll deductions in much the same way you view taxes and other deductions, if any, such as insurance premiums. They are necessary deductions. The money is gone. It's not in your paycheck; so you don't have it to spend.

If your employer doesn't offer payroll deduction, be sure to make your IRA deposit first, before paying any other bills. That's easy to say and very hard to do. Too hard for most people. The temptation to spend it all is too overwhelming. If you don't have a 401(k), you really must get a checking account and have your IRA make automatic monthly drafts on your checking account. If it becomes too hard to make ends meet at the end of the month, then make a reduction in the amount of the monthly draft.

Payroll deduction or automatic draft from your checking account "hides" your money at the outset. It's very important that the money continues to be hidden in such a way that you don't often notice it. If you notice the money frequently, the temptation to spend it prematurely will be very strong. Savers frequently see their checking account statements and passbook savings accounts. For that reason alone, these accounts are not suitable for your long-term savings. Additionally, passbook accounts are unsuitable because they are too accessible.

A Balanced Plan

Here's an abbreviated example of balancing all your goals.

Take home pay for the month		$1700
IRA or 401(k) contribution	$150	
Rent	450	
Medical	100	
Heat, electricity, water	100	
Telephone	40	
Car note	200	
Payment of other debt	150	
Medium-term savings	<u>50</u>	
Subtotal		1240
Balance		$460

Notice that paying yourself first is at the top of the list of expenses. It's the most important. That IRA or 401(k) contribution goes toward your long-term goals. The $460 is the amount of money left over for the entire month to cover the other expenses (food, gasoline, entertainment, clothes, etc.). It becomes an automatic budget, or limit, to spend on everything else. Part of the $460 per month will wind up as spare change in a jar at the end of each day. That money can be used for short-term goals.

After your car note is paid off, put $200 per month into a separate savings account. That way, you can make a bigger down payment on your next car. Hopefully, in the long term, you'll be able to pay cash for your cars in the future. In any case, continue to make car payments to yourself when you're not making them to the auto finance company. In addition to a car account, you may want another account for medium-term needs. I recommend an account for vacation expenses plus otherwise unplanned expenses, such as big ticket emergency expenses. Put a small amount into this account each month. Without a savings account for these type expenses, such as major dental work, a new central heating unit, etc., it's all too easy to get in debt and stay there for a long time.

The above example provides funds for today's needs, for medium-term needs (the car fund), and for long-term goals. It provides balance and puts you in control of your finances. Of course, each person's situation will be different and each person will want to reevaluate and adjust the plan periodically.

Obviously, paying yourself first results in less money available for everything else. You could delay any spending cuts until you run out of money near the end of the month or pay period. But there are much better ways to make ends meet. In the next chapter we'll look at painless ways to save money.

CHAPTER 5

HAVING FUN SAVING MONEY

Spending vs. Savings

If saving money is such a good idea, why are so many people up to their ears in debt? Why has it been more popular to spend than to save? A look at the economic history of the United States since the 1930s provides some answers.

Most Americans who grew up during the Great Depression of the 1930s experienced poverty. They witnessed drastic price declines in financial assets, price declines in goods and services, and sharp declines in their incomes. They acquired a deep-seated attachment to the values of money and hard work. They closed the gap between what they wanted and what they bought in the only way possible at that time – they wanted less.

Rising inflation after World War II changed all that. In the 1960s and 1970s, the American way changed from saving to spending. A penny saved was no longer a penny earned, as the purchasing power of money declined sharply. People became eager to buy today because tomorrow prices would be higher. It was smart to borrow money to purchase consumer goods because the interest expense (fully tax-deductible then) was less than the rate of inflation. The economic system thus rewarded spenders and penalized savers. This economic shift created a dramatic change in personalities between generations. Depression era old-timers wouldn't spend a dollar, while their adult children wouldn't save a dollar. Borrowing and spending became the American way.

Now in the latter part of the 1990s, American households as well as the federal government are deeply in debt. Inflation has been dramatically reduced, and consumer interest expense is no longer tax deductible. These factors alone now give the advantage to savers. When those factors are added to the job insecurities of the 1990s and the bleak outlook for the old Social Security program, you get substantial benefits to savers and a tough situation for borrowers.

What is Savings?

But what does it mean to save money? Do you save money by using coupons in the supermarket? Do you save money by switching to a long distance telephone company with lower rates? The answer is yes and no to both questions. Yes, you save money in the sense that you reduce your per unit expense. However, if you increase your volume of consumption, you do not save money. If you normally spend 100 minutes on long distance telephone service each month at 25 cents per minute, your bill is $25.00. Would you save money by switching to a different company charging 15 cents per minute? Yes, if you only talked 100 minutes after the switch. If you talked 200 minutes after the switch, you would save no money at all. In fact, your expense would go up from $25 to $30 a month.

If you talked the usual 100 minutes after the telephone company switch, you saved $10. For that $10 to be true savings, so to speak, it must be invested in such a way that its value will grow. Savings invested in a boat or a car is not true savings because those assets depreciate in value over time. Savings invested in a house generally qualifies if the house is properly maintained and owned for many years. Similarly, your own business enterprise could be a good savings vehicle if it provides net income. One particularly excellent savings vehicle is mutual funds, which are more fully explained in Chapter 8.

The Burden of Debt

Being in debt makes it so much harder to achieve your future needs and goals. That's true because so much of your future income is paid out in interest expense. Without the burden of that interest expense, you could have so much more with your current income. You may say yes that's true, but I don't want to wait until I have the cash to buy what I want. Besides, I'll pay off the debt in so many years and then be able to buy more things that I want. So why wait? Why not get into debt? Isn't that the American way? Certainly, debt makes sense in some situations, such as buying a house and financing a college education. However, carrying debt from month to month is not the best way to finance consumer purchases. Because of the interest expense on debt financing, you wind up paying far too much for what you can afford. Get ahead (out of debt) and you can afford to have more.

If you're now in debt, you'll find that paying off your debts is a freeing experience. You'll enjoy the comfort of knowing that you can afford what you are buying. Avoiding debt can also reduce stress and marital friction.

Many people temporarily raise their lifestyle by going into debt, only to find out that the burden of debt controls their lifestyle. If debt is a problem for you, get personalized counseling. If you're married and in debt, both of you should get counseling. Most major cities have nonprofit organizations which will help you to reduce your expenses and pay off your debts. Check the yellow pages under credit and debt counseling services. United Way sponsors Consumer Credit Counseling Service (CCCS) which has branches in most major cities. To find a branch in your area, call 1-800-388-CCCS.

If you're in debt, CCCS can serve as a middleman between you and your creditors to reach a mutually agreeable plan to pay off your debts. Thus, the CCCS can help get the bill collectors off your back. Even if you're not in debt, CCCS can counsel you in how to reduce your living expenses in order to increase your savings.

Avoid the Credit Card Blues

Excessive spending with credit cards gets more people into financial trouble than anything else. In addition to paying more for everything because of interest expense, being in debt limits a person's ability to provide for long-term goals.

If overspending on credit cards is a problem for you, the best thing you can do is quit using credit cards. Of course, that's a huge step for anyone who has used credit cards for more than a year! One very good way to ease into this credit card withdrawal is to put your cards into a safe deposit box. If you don't have a safe deposit box, then freeze the cards, literally. Put the cards in a plastic container, fill the container with water, and then put the container in your freezer or freezer section of the refrigerator. When there comes a time in the future that you need to charge an expensive item, thaw out the card the night before you need it. You'll still have the card when and if you need it. After using the card, refreeze it. By using this method, you'll be forced to either do without or pay cash because unfreezing the card is too much trouble for a small or medium purchase. That's the whole point, of course. Using this technique will drastically reduce the use (overuse) of the card. To the extent that your reaction is to do without, you will automatically reduce your expenses. If you do have cash to pay for what you would have charged on the card, you might reconsider how important that purchase is, whether you really need it, and whether you need to keep your cash for something more important later in the day or week.

If you do want to use your credit card regularly, then charge only what you can pay for in full when the bill comes in. When the bill comes, pay all the current charges plus the finance charge. In addition, pay something toward reducing the balance to zero. In subsequent months, continue to reduce the unpaid balance until the balance is zero.

Another approach some people use is to deduct each charge slip from their checking account as they make the charge. In your check register you would put "CC" for credit card in the space reserved for the check number. Obviously, you would then quit charging anything when your checking account balance reached zero or reached a certain minimum level.

If you carry no balance on your credit card each month, get a card with little or no annual fee. If you do carry over an unpaid balance from one month to another, get a card with the lowest interest rate available. Each month, pay all the interest expense and gradually pay down the balance to zero. At the same time, make monthly contributions to your long-term fund. When credit cards are paid off, increase contributions to the long-term fund.

Save on "Success"

We all want to feel successful. Success means different things to different people. For some people, success means doing your job to the best of your ability. It could also mean raising children who are happy, loving, decent people. Certainly, there are several other definitions of success. One measure of success is owning expensive status symbols, such as a new sports car or a home in the most affluent section of town. Many others who can't afford these status symbols seek less expensive status symbols, such as the most expensive brands of blue jeans or shoes. There's nothing wrong with owning these things, but too many people get in over their heads when they try to impress friends or family members with their material possessions.

Owning expensive status symbols is not very satisfying in the long-run for those heavily in debt. It's also not a good way to become wealthy. The 1996 book *The Millionaire Next Door* by authors Stanley and Danko has documented that most millionaires do not drive expensive new cars and live in fabulous homes. Instead, they live modestly and save a significant percentage of their incomes.

These millionaires are well satisfied with their possessions and enjoy the feeling of being in control of their financial destinies. They are interested in their own goals. They are not driven by status or materialistic competition with others. For these people, success is more about who they are on the inside than what they have to show others on the outside. Saving on status symbols can be a major ingredient in your becoming a millionaire.

Sex Appeal for Singles

Dating can be expensive for both men and women. A nice apartment, fashionable clothes, a sharp looking car, and plenty of money for recreation are very important for most young, single people. For many people, it seems to be nearly impossible to have all those things plus a long-term savings account. If something has to wait until later, the savings account has to wait. Certainly, sex appeal now is more important than a lot of money later.

However, nothing has to wait until later. If you pay yourself first, as described in the earlier chapter, you will still have sufficient money for spending now. In fact, I believe that contributing to a 401(k) plan will actually increase your appeal to the opposite sex. Why? Intelligent women who are aware of the benefits of 401(k) plans will be very favorably impressed by men who are taking advantage of tax-deferred growth plus employer matching contributions. These women appreciate men who make prudent plans for the future as well as the present. Likewise, intelligent men who are aware of the benefits of 401(k) plans will be favorably impressed by women who are taking advantage of those benefits.

As stated in Chapter 3, it is imperative to start saving now, not later. You can have it all - optimum benefits now and in the future.

Car Savings

You can probably save more money on transportation than on any other category of expense. Most of us need a car. However, some people, particularly in large, metropolitan areas, don't really need one. So first, consider whether or not you really need one.

Does public transportation go near your place of work? If so, can you find a place to live that is within walking distance of the bus or train stop? Ideally, you would also be within walking or bicycling distance of stores, restaurants, etc. If public transportation to work is not feasible, what about car pooling as a rider with another worker? On weekends when you want to go where public transportation doesn't go, you could rent a car or catch a cab.

If you live with a spouse, does each of you really need your own car? Two cars are much more expensive than one car. Look at what your real needs are. A small decrease in convenience by switching from two cars to one car could produce very substantial savings. That savings could provide far greater benefits to you in the long run than the small decrease in your current convenience benefit.

If you're like most of us, you'll decide that you really do need a car or maybe two cars for the family. In any case, you can very substantially reduce your transportation expenses by making wise car buying decisions.

Paying cash for your new or used car can save you a lot of money. For example, a $14,000 car note paid in 48 monthly installments at 9.5% interest costs $2,896 in interest expense. Of course, most of us have to finance car purchases. However, when you finish paying off the note, keep the car for as long as you can, and make car payments to yourself. Each time you replace your car, the goal is to substantially reduce the amount you have to borrow by making a larger down payment. In the long-run, you can save a lot of money in interest expense this way.

Paying cash also provides the ability to reduce your car insurance expense. Once you own your car, you can drop the expensive collision coverage. When the car is more than four or five years old, it's generally cost effective to drop the collision coverage.

More important than the financing and insurance savings is the kind of car you get. Do you need a top of the line sports car? Do you need a full sized car when everything and everybody will fit into a smaller car? Do you need a new car?

Obviously, you can buy a used car for much less than the cost of a new one. Is the used car a better deal? It is if you pay no more than a fair price for the quality you get. Fortunately, the quality of cars has improved substantially in the last decade or two. On average, new cars have fewer defects than they used to have. Properly maintained, used cars last longer and need fewer repairs than they did in the 1960s and 1970s. Late model cars are built so well nowadays that you don't need to be an expert or part-time mechanic to get a long life from your car. With reasonable care, you can expect a car to last more than 100,000 miles. If you decide on a used car and you're not an auto mechanic, look for cars which have a good reliability record (those which historically need fewer than average repairs). To check reliability, get "Consumer Reports" magazine annual auto issue published in April of each year. It profiles new cars and provides frequency of repair information for used cars. Next, go to the library and get the most recent issue of "N.A.D.A. Official Used Car Guide" or "N.A.D.A. Older Used Car Guide" to determine approximate prices of the several cars you have chosen for reliability. Another source of pricing information is "Kelly's Blue Book," available on the Internet at **www.kbb.com**. Next, shop for a few of these cars. Of course, some of the cars you'll see might be pieces of junk which look O.K. at first glance. In that regard, be sure to look at the cars in sunlight so that you can more easily see any defects or damage. Once you find a car which is priced right, have a mechanic examine the car for you before you buy it. Incidentally, there are a few companies whose sole business is examining used cars for potential car buyers. Look under Auto Inspection or Auto Diagnostic in the Yellow Pages of the phone book for a large city. When looking for a good used car, consider relatives and friends, classified newspaper ads, auto auctions, car dealers, and the Internet. Also, new cars are now being marketed on the Internet.

In addition to "Consumer Reports" and the N.A.D.A. book, there are a few more sources of information that may be helpful. See "Money" magazine's annual Car Buyers Guide in March for information on new car costs and maintenance. The National

Highway Traffic Safety Administration has an online database on the Internet at **www.nhtsa.dot.gov**. Anyone with information on a vehicle's make, model, and year can search recall records, defect investigations, and consumer complaints in NHTSA's files, for free. Additionally, there is at least one private firm which helps used car buyers to verify a car's history. The company is Carfax Vehicle History Services of Fairfax, Va. The company maintains a nationwide database on 190 million previously owned vehicles. The company's database comes from state motor vehicle agencies and other sources. With the VIN (vehicle identification number) of the car, the database shows if the car title is encumbered by liens, or if it has been wrecked, damaged by flood, salvaged, recalled by government or manufacturer, or bought back by an automaker under a state's "lemon laws." The company also provides odometer reading checks. Of course, the company's records are not perfect, but the company does offer a very interesting service for used car buyers. Cost is $19.50. Carfax is on the Internet at **www.carfaxreport.com/**.

I recommend several other Internet addresses to car buyers. Excellent, free information on new and used cars and trucks can be found at **www.edmunds.com**. A free book on used car buying is located at **www.goodasnew.com/**.

Estimated cost per mile is the most critical financial factor in evaluating a car, new or used. You could figure the cost per mile over the entire time you plan to keep the car, or you could do the calculation for each year that you plan to own the car. It's easier to do the calculations once for the estimated total life of the car rather than for each year you plan to own the car.

First calculate the combined cost of financing charges plus depreciation. Don't let these math formulas bother you. They are easy to understand. Car A is the car you're buying. The line numbers correspond to the more comprehensive formula for all costs, which is in Appendix C.

FORMULA FOR CALCULATING ESTIMATED FINANCING AND DEPRECIATION COST:
Line 15a Down payment plus trade-in, or cash price of car A
Line 15b Balance to finance
Line 15c Monthly payment
Line 15d Number of months to pay
Line 15e Total monthly payments. Line 15c times Line 15d
Line 15f Cost of car including financing. Line 15a + Line 15e
Line 17 Estimated future trade-in value of Car A
Line 19 Estimated net cost of car A. Line 15f - Line 17
Line 20 Estimated cost per mile. Line 19 divided by estimated miles
         to be driven.

The following example will illustrate the entire calculation. Let's say you're buying a three-year-old car in April 1996 with 36,000 miles on it. You plan to drive the car for nine more years, at which time it will have approximately 144,000 miles on it. Your price for the car including sales tax is $8500 (Line 15f). According to your calculations (explained below), the ending value of the car (Line 17) will be approximately $800. The estimated net cost of the car (Line 19) is ($8500 - $800) or $7700. In this example, $7700 is the total depreciation expense of the car. Estimated miles to be driven is (144,000 - 36,000) or 108,000 miles. The estimated cost per mile is ($7700 / 108,000 miles) or about seven cents per mile (Line 20).

Here's how to calculate estimated ending value. When you sell the car, it will be twelve years old. See what that twelve year old model is worth now. In April 1996, a twelve-year-old car would be a 1984 car. Use the current "NADA Older Used Car Guide" to find out the value of that 1984 model. If that model was not in existence in 1984, look up similar 1984 models with approximately the same original cost. The trade-in value of the 1984 model per the guide book above is $800. We'll assume that when you sell the 1993 model nine years from now, the value will be about the same $800. To get the value for Line 15a above (if there's a trade-in), simply look up its trade-in value in the current NADA book.

For most people, the above calculations are sufficient to compare the cost of one car to another car. Appendix C provides an enlarged formula in case you want to incorporate gasoline, insurance, maintenance, repairs, and parking expenses into the calculation. Of course, the cost of repairs is the most difficult to estimate. One way to deal with the cost of repairs is to estimate major repairs for used cars more than three years old and only routine maintenance for new cars less than three years old.

Using the suggested format in Appendix C, I've compared the estimated cost of three new medium sized cars over a nine-year period to the cost of one used medium sized car over the same period. To determine trade-in values on the cars, I took a small sample of intermediate or medium sized models of domestic cars. Since models are discontinued or changed, I had to compare similar models in the NADA book. I estimated new car prices at 8 percent discount from the manufacturers' suggested retail price (MSRP), and I estimated future inflation of car prices at 4 percent per year. In this example, I estimated costs of buying a used 1993 car in 1996 and keeping it for nine years until the year 2005. I compared that cost to the estimated costs of buying a new 1996 car, trading it for a new 1999 car, and trading the 1999 car for a 2002 car, and then selling that car in 2005. The charts in Appendix C show the details of the calculations.

In this example, including insurance, gas, maintenance and financing, the used car would cost 27 cents per mile for 108,000 miles vs. 52 cents per mile for 108,000 miles for the new cars. Total estimated savings over the nine-year period is about $27,000, or about $250 per month. Those savings alone don't enable you to accumulate $1,000,000. The wise investment of those savings over a long enough period of years could enable you to be a millionaire, as discussed in Chapter 3. In this example, we'll say $200 per month of the savings goes into a 401(k) plan. $200 per month growing at 12% per year accumulates to $37,767 at the end of nine years. If that money (no additional out of pocket contributions) grows at 12% compounded annually, it will amount to $642,035 after an additional 25 years. If your employer has a dollar for dollar match in your 401(k) plan, you'll have $75,533 after nine years and $1,284,070 after the additional 25 years.

Many good cars experience price deprecation of about half their cost in only three years. After about the fourth year, depreciation stays relatively low and repair expenses increase. So, you can get a very nice looking three to a five-year-old car at a substantial savings. You'll have plenty left over to go out and have fun. We're not really talking about deprivation or sacrifice here.

For many people, the best idea is to purchase a new car with cash and keep the car for ten to twelve years. This is smart shopping for transportation. That smart shopping can save cash for your other needs. With a portion of those savings, **pay yourself first**.

Save on Housing

Many young single people have the flexibility to fund a $1 million payoff by making wise choices on their housing. Generally speaking, a young single person has these housing options: buy a place to live alone or with others, rent a place to live alone or with others, live with parents. Usually, the last choice is the least expensive. Of course, many young adults would rather not live with their parents; so let's consider the alternatives. By sharing rent with one, two, or three roommates or house mates, you may be able to put aside $300 per month. It's essential that you must pay yourself first with that $300 per month, or at least pay yourself a major part of that $300 savings.

This savings strategy need not be a pain or unduly burdensome. On the contrary, it could improve your lifestyle with additional friends and acquaintances. For a few people, this arrangement could last a lifetime. Most of you will change your housing situation within several years. Nevertheless, if you can save $300 per month for just five years, here are the results assuming a 12% annual compounded return on your savings.

Current Age	Amount at 55	Amount at 65
22	$581,735	$1,806,781
25	414,067	1,286,031
30	234,953	729,728
35	133,319	414,067

In all cases, your out-of-pocket investment is $300 per month times 60 months = $18,000. What a deal for a 22-year-old! By living with new friends for five years, you save $18,000 which turns into a $581,743 bonanza on your 55th birthday and into $1,806,802 if you keep it invested until age 65, earning 12% annually. At 10% growth, the results would be $334,118 at age 55 and $868,608 at age 65 for the 22-year-old. Of course, the above example assumes the money grows in a tax deferred account, such as a 401(k).

Reduce Your Income Taxes

Numerous credits and deductions are available in various situations. The income tax laws are so complex that you may want to hire a professional to prepare your tax return, particularly if you have income other than that reported on a W-2 form. If you have only W-2 income, few deductions, no child-care expenses, no earned income credits (explained below), and no other complications, you'll probably be better off to prepare your own tax return and save the tax return preparation fee. In any case, don't wait until after year-end to see how you can lower your taxes. Obviously, I can't begin to cover all or most of the available credits and deductions in this book. However, one or more of the following suggestions may save you thousands of dollars in taxes.

Shift deductions in order to itemize every other year

Most people have more control over their deductions than over their income. If you are paid wages before the end of the year, those wages are taxable in the current year, regardless of whether you cash the check before or after year-end. On the other hand, you can prepay next year's expenses before the end of the year and get the deductions in the current year. Prepaying expenses (accelerating deductions) works for you only when you are able to itemize expenses, as opposed to taking the standard deduction.

If your actual deductible expenses are only slightly less than the standard deduction each year, you may be able to save taxes by carefully timing your deductible expenses. Many people are able to bunch certain expenses every other year in order to itemize expenses every other year for greater total deductions on the two tax returns. In other words, you alternate taking higher itemized deductions in one year and the standard deduction the following year. Consider what you can do in this regard by manipulating tax and charity expenses from one year to another. We'll use 1997 and 1998 in the hypothetical example. Pay your last installment of 1997 state income taxes in 1998. Then pay your last instalment of 1998 taxes by Dec. 31, 1998. Similarly, double up on property taxes, if possible. Some counties will allow payment of 1997 taxes by the following January 31 without any penalty. In such a case, pay the 1997 taxes in January of 1998 and pay 1998 property taxes by December 31, 1998. Additionally, wait until January 1998 to make charitable contributions that you would ordinarily make by December 1997. In 1998 make your normal contributions plus prepay some of what you would ordinarily contribute in early 1999. This strategy bunches expenses in 1998 and even years. It's a worthwhile strategy if it enables you to itemize for the greater deductions in 1998 while taking the standard deduction in the odd years.

Earned income credit (EIC)

The EIC is a credit for certain workers earning less than a specified income. It reduces the tax you owe and may give you a refund, even if you don't owe any tax. If you don't have a qualifying child, the specified income is $10,030 for 1998. If you have one qualifying child, the specified income is $26,473 ($30,095 if you have more than one qualifying child). The tax credit can be as much as $341 without a qualifying child, or as much as $2,271 to $3,756, depending on the number of qualifying children. You must see the IRS instructions for the definition of a qualifying child and for exceptions and special rules. Certainly, this can be a very substantial benefit to qualifying taxpayers. If your income is below these specified levels, check out the current instructions. The rules and specified income levels are subject to change each year. So realize that you might qualify now, even with income greater than the amounts specified above.

Child and dependent care expenses

If you paid someone to care for your child or other qualifying person so you and your spouse (if filing a joint return) could work or look for work, you may be able to take the credit for child and dependent care expenses. See IRS instructions for Form 2441 to see if you qualify.

Other tax-savings strategies

If you have children and also have investment assets, you can cut some income taxes by gifting assets to your children using the Uniform Gifts to Minors Act. The investment income earned on these assets is taxed to the child. For more details, read the instructions for federal tax Form 8615, or ask your tax advisor. In all tax matters, read the current instructions because the rules change so frequently.

Have your employer withhold enough from your payroll checks so that you won't owe interest and penalties for underpayment of taxes during the year.

Most importantly, contribute as much as you can to individual retirement accounts (IRAs), 401(k) plans, and other tax-deductible retirement plans. If you are self employed, contribute to the equivalent plans for the self employed, such as the Keogh Plan. The importance of retirement plan contributions cannot be overstated.

Small Savings Add Up

Here are a few ideas to reduce your living expenses. Some of these ideas will work for you; some won't work for you. You must decide what works best for you.

- Shop in supermarkets and discount stores when they have the same quality products as the higher priced stores.

- If you need an item only very rarely, consider renting it, rather than buying it. If you buy, the product may rust or become obsolete by the time you need it again.

- Save on used items. For instance, on used furniture you can save a lot of money, often 50 to 80 percent. When shopping for a chest of drawers a few years ago, I bought a very nice solid wood chest in a used furniture store that cost quite a bit less than a particle board chest in a new furniture store. Besides, the solid wood chest had far superior quality. Some thrift stores sell a wide variety of high quality merchandise, not just clothes.

- Consider using repair and upholstery shops for major appliances and furniture. Maybe the item is worth fixing, rather than replacing.

- Brown bag more of your lunches. If you currently buy all of your lunches at restaurants, try brown bagging once a week. Have fun each week on your brown bag day. On some weeks, you could have a nice, peaceful time eating in a nearby park. On other weeks, you might eat quickly and spend the rest of your lunch period window shopping, browsing in the nearest branch library, or doing whatever else you want to do. Many libraries have interesting programs at noon. Reducing expenses doesn't have to be boring. It can be fun.

If you already brown bag occasionally, consider adding one more day per week. Over the period of a year, the cumulative savings can be substantial. Saving just $5 a week on lunches adds up to $250 per year. If you brown bag several times a week, you'll save much more. Add up how much you spend each week for lunches. You'll probably be surprised. However, remember that moderation is important here, as in most areas of life. Don't brown bag every day. Reward yourself on paydays and special occasions. Most of us who work inside buildings need to splurge and eat out at least once a week. If your savings program is boring, you'll eventually, in the not too distant future, quit it altogether. So have fun while you save.

A budget is not essential if your pay yourself first. However, it can be very helpful to review a few categories of expenses in order to identify areas where you can free up some money. Consider how much you spend on sodas, cigarettes, alcohol, snacks, clothes, fast food, lunches at restaurants, etc. Most likely, you already know which area or areas might be a problem for you. If you are spending excessively in one area, consider limiting yourself in that area to a fixed amount per month. Little savings mount up. See Table 5-1 on page 77 for the results of saving as little as $25 per week.

Telephone service

Save money on long distance telephone calls. Take advantage of the lower weekend and evening rates. We're all bombarded with media messages to change to the newest plan of each of the long distance carriers. It can be worth your while to investigate the rate structure of several telephone companies. In order to keep the investigation as easy and simple as possible, contact your current company and no more than two or three others. Get their rates including any flat charges per month, minimum bill per month, and per call surcharge, if any. Most will charge so much per minute interstate and so much per minute intrastate, regardless of distance called. Others charge according to distance in miles from your city to the called city. Most offer weekend and evening discounts. Once you have the rate structures in hand, determine what your typical monthly bill would cost with each company. The lowest cost company for you may be different from your next door neighbor. If there is a volume discount, do you generate that much volume each month? If not, take that absence of a discount into consideration. Finally, does the difference in costs among the different companies justify switching? Generally, the few largest companies have their own cables. The smaller companies buy excess capacity from those large companies which have their own cables. You may like the service better with your present company even though you could save a little money elsewhere. You have to evaluate that for yourself.

One additional point about long distance calling plans. When a company introduces a new plan, it does not automatically shift old customers to that plan. You have to request it. The company introduces the new plan not to lower revenues from existing customers but to entice the customers of its competitors to switch carriers. In fact, if you are a current customer of a company with a new plan, the company may actually discourage you from switching to the new plan. When I called and asked about switching plans with my current company, the representative advised me to keep the old plan. Against that recommendation, I told the representative to switch me to the new plan after I had compared costs of the two plans. The new plan saves me about $10 per month.

Public transportation

Ride public transportation to work or car pool with co-workers. Realize that your cost of driving to work is much more than the cost of gasoline and parking. When you buy car insurance, the agent asks you if the car is driven to and from work or used only for pleasure. The reason is that insurance rates are higher for cars driven to and from work. Additionally, cars wear out and need repairs on the basis of miles driven. New tires, engine tuneups, etc. are needed in addition to the gasoline burned in driving to work. Once you compare the costs of public transportation to cost of driving to work, you may find the difference is quite substantial.

Of course, there are other factors to consider as well. Taking your own car provides the convenience of a totally flexible schedule. But switching to public transportation is not all pain. You'll be able to relax on the way home. You won't have to fight the 5:00 P.M. traffic. You'll be able to come home in a more receptive mood to greet the family and interact with them. They'll be less need for immediately "unwinding" upon returning home.

Win Big With Fewer Lottery Tickets

In the standard state lotto game you win the jackpot if you correctly name all six numbers which are randomly picked. In Texas, the numbers are from one to 50. Your chance to win is about one in 16 million. You have a much better chance of being killed by a lightning strike. According to the National Safety Council, those odds were one in 4,524,912 as of 1993, the latest figures available. That's killed, not just struck by lightning. Most people struck by lightning survive the strike.

If you purchase 26 lottery tickets each week, your odds of winning are less than two in a million each week. Those odds are obviously very remote. If you reduce the number of lottery tickets you buy, you'll almost surely come out a big winner! For example, if you reduce your weekly lottery tickets from 26 to one, you would still have a chance to win the lottery; plus, you could invest the remaining $25 per week. Big deal! You'll never get rich saving $25 per week, right? Wrong. $25 per week is $1300 per year. $1300 per year can grow to a nice jackpot given a good rate of return and some time. Assuming that your investment grows in a tax-deferred retirement account, here's what your jackpot would look like assuming 12% annual compound growth. Deposit is made at the end of each year.

Table 5-1

Year	Out of pocket investment	Cumulative value year-end
1	$1,300	$1,300
5	6,500	8,259
10	13,000	22,813
15	19,500	48,464
20	26,000	93,668
25	32,500	173,334
30	39,000	313,732
35	45,500	561,163
40	52,000	997,219

Saving money for 40 years sounds like a drag, right? Even 10 years seems like an eternity. Then don't set your goals for so long. Put this plan into effect for just seven years and see what happens. At the end of the seventh year, stop making new contributions and just let the balance grow through reinvestment of the gains in the account. At the end of year seven, your out-of-pocket investment of $9,100 would be worth $13,116. A mere rock slide. At year 40, it would be worth $552,073, and at year 45 it would be worth $972,941, assuming 12 percent compounded growth. Another avalanche!

If wagering on the lottery is fun for you, buy one ticket on each payday. Put the rest of what you were paying for tickets into savings. Pay this amount to yourself first! If you really do want a jackpot, that's the realistic way of getting one.

What Comes First?

Pay yourself first. This can't be overemphasized. The savings ideas in this chapter can help you determine how much to pay yourself. If you can free up some substantial savings in transportation or housing, then you can pay yourself substantially. If not, pay yourself first a small amount through payroll deduction. You'll automatically cut back on what's least important in order to make ends meet. Or, if you get a raise in salary, you won't need to cut back a thing. Just put the wage increase into savings and continue to live as before. Doing it this way makes saving money painless.

Table 5-2
Amount Needed Annually at Beginning of year to Accumulate $1,000,000 at age 65.

Your age	25	30	35	40	45	50
Growth						
6%	6,096	8,466	11,933	25,646	25,646	40,530
8%	3,574	5,373	8,173	20,233	20,233	34,102
10%	2,054	3,354	5,527	15,873	15,873	28,612
12%	1,164	2,068	3,700	12,392	12,392	23,893

Is $1 million enough?

Appendix D provides two tables which help to answer the question is $1 million enough. One table shows how much $1 million will be worth in today's dollars when you reach age 65, after inflation adjustments. The next table in the appendix shows how much you need to accumulate to provide an inflation adjusted equivalent of $35,000 per year in income after retirement using certain assumptions. If you review these tables in Appendix D, you might decide that $1 million is not going to provide as much purchasing power as you would like. You may want to adjust your goal higher. Appendix D also provides compound interest tables in case you want to do some personal calculations.

Right now, you can't know for sure whether $1,000,000 is too much or too little for your future goals. Small variances in the rate of inflation and the rate of compounded growth produce very large variances in total dollar values over a long period of time. It's best to make conservative estimates of investment growth and inflation. The problem is that economists can only provide a wide range of estimates for us to use to calculate investment growth and inflation. The best most of us can do is to save as much as we reasonably can without harsh sacrifices (hopefully from 6% to 15% of income). Then invest the savings to get as high a rate of return as possible without taking on too much risk.

By following the principles of this book, you can have your cake and eat it too. You can enjoy today and save for a much more rewarding tomorrow. While you're saving for tomorrow, visualize the enjoyment you will have when you reach your future goals. The visualization of those future goals can bring a sense of satisfaction now, and then again later, when your goals are outwardly manifested. If you don't have specific goals in mind, then visualize the peace and contentment of financial independence. Believe that whatever you decide to do, within reason, you'll be able to do.

CHAPTER 6

IS THERE A GUARANTEE?

There is no guarantee that your savings and investment program will accomplish your goals. Any one of several things could cause your plan to fail.

A natural or man made disaster could wipe out an entire region of the country, or even devastate the entire country. Such potential disasters include floods, nuclear explosions, volcanoes, a large meteor striking the earth, etc. Any of these things could wreak havoc and kill thousands or millions of people. These things are possible but most unlikely in our lifetimes.

Financial markets could crash, similar to the 1930s. It's possible, but again, very unlikely. Economists have much greater knowledge now about how to prevent such a thing and how to recover if it did happen. Additionally, numerous automatic safeguards are built into our system now to prevent another great depression. Probably the biggest risk to an excellent savings and investment plan is short-sighted government policy.

Government's Affect on Your Wealth

The federal government, including the Federal Reserve Board, could make disastrous decisions affecting the economy. Government decisions strongly affect the rate of inflation. Runaway inflation could destroy the value of our savings. Even moderately high inflation over a period of years greatly diminishes the value of savings. Appendix D illustrates what inflation can do to the purchasing power of $1,000,000. Fortunately, inflation is modest at the current time. Additionally, it's possible to minimize the effects of inflation by purchasing those things which have little or no inflation. Just because average inflation is, say, 4% per year doesn't mean the things that you buy increase 4% per year. Indeed televisions, computers, some foods, etc. have increased very little or even decreased over the last few years. While the Consumer Price Index may increase 4%, the things you buy might increase only 1% or 2%. Thus, the value of your savings would be based on 1% or 2% inflation.

Confiscatory taxes are another potential problem that could ruin your savings plan. Confiscatory taxes are taxes which are so high that you have little purchasing power left after paying the taxes. Now, we don't have that problem. It's unlikely that voters will accept confiscatory taxes. Nevertheless, some tax increases will most likely be necessary within the next decade or two. With a projected increased percentage of people living past retirement age in the years between 2020 and 2030, the demands on government for retirement income, medical care, and so forth will likely skyrocket. At that time there will be a relatively low percentage of workers paying income and payroll taxes to support those needs. Either substantial changes will be made in the meantime, or those workers will likely have to pay higher taxes to meet the needs of government.

What's needed is for the government to balance short-term needs and long-term needs. It's all too easy to see short-term problems which might be improved if only the government spent more money on them. However, too many politicians overlook the need to prepare for the long-term problems, problems beyond the next one or two elections. There has to be a balance between short-term goals and long-term goals.

Fortunately, the American economy is strong and resilient. Government leaders can easily be changed by the voters if those leaders go far astray. Eventually, we can hope and expect that our leaders well make appropriate compromises in order to prevent runaway inflation, depression, or confiscatory taxes.

Outstanding Opportunity

Just as the government must balance short-term goals and long-term goals, so too, must we do the same as individuals to achieve maximum success. Whatever happens to inflation and taxes, it still makes sense to save and invest for the future. We can't know for sure what the future holds. No, you can't count on 15% or 12% or even 10% growth in the stock market. Even if future rates of return become low by current standards, your tax deferred retirement accounts will still make good sense due to the magic of compound growth. If all goes well, you will still be in good enough health and have enough financial resources to enjoy a lifestyle which will surpass what you have previously experienced.

Any kind of IRA, even a nondeductible IRA, is an outstanding opportunity. The 401(k) is usually an even better opportunity if your employer makes matching contributions. The matching contributions amount to a raise in pay. Even if you are currently living paycheck to paycheck, you can afford to make a 401(k) or an IRA contribution by paying yourself first. So sign up for an IRA, a 401(k), or both plans. Do it now and give yourself the chance to:

Become a Millionaire in Your Current Job!

CHAPTER 7

INVESTMENT OPTIONS FOR YOUR 401(k) or IRA

Creditor vs. Owner Investments

When you invest money, you become either a creditor or an owner. A creditor lends money to an organization (bank, corporation, government, etc.). Most people usually think of creditors as banks or finance companies that lend money to people. However, it also works the other way. People lend money to banks and other organizations. For example, a savings account is a loan from you to the bank. That savings account is your investment. When you make the loan to an organization or bank, the borrower gives you a Certificate of Deposit (CD), a bond, a mortgage, or other evidence of the debt.

Except for bank savings and checking accounts, when you lend money to an organization, the debtor promises to pay back your money to you at a specific future date, the maturity date. On that date the security expires or matures, and the borrower must pay back the entire amount of the loan. During the time that the borrower holds and uses your money for its own purposes, it will pay you a certain percentage of interest income on your investment. With bank savings and checking accounts, the loan (your deposit) has no specific maturity date.

Interest income is sort of like rent. The borrower is renting the use of your money for a period of time. During the period of time the borrower uses your money, the borrower pays you rent in the form of interest income.

If all borrowers paid the same interest rate, we would want to lend money only to the borrower that could guarantee to pay us back, no matter what happened to the economy. In the USA, the safest debtor is considered to be the U.S. Government. The government has the power to tax and to confiscate property if taxes are not paid. So, most people believe the government will always be able to pay back its debts. Now, if we would rather lend money to the government than lend money to a businessman opening a hardware store in town, how is the businessman going to be able to borrow money? There's more risk that the hardware store will fail. Therefore, to compensate investors for the greater risk, the hardware store has to pay a higher return to its creditors than the government has to pay to its creditors. The safer the investment, the lower the return. The greater the risk, the greater the return demanded by the investors.

Being a creditor is less risky than being an owner. That's because the creditor must be paid all the interest income due before the owner can receive any dividends on the investment. An owner has the opportunity to earn high returns because once the expenses (including interest expenses) are paid, the owner keeps all the net income. That's true even if the net income is many times the interest expense. Since risk is higher for owners, owners expect a higher return. Since risk is lower for creditors, they expect a lower return. There are numerous types of creditor investments including bank accounts; bank CDs; U.S. Treasury bills, notes, and bonds; municipal bonds; corporate bonds; mortgages; fixed annuities; and Guaranteed Investment Contracts.

Owner investments consist primarily of common stocks or investments which own common stocks, such as mutual funds.

Bank Accounts, CDs and GICs

When we deposit money in the bank, we don't think of ourselves as creditors lending money to the bank. Yet, that's exactly what happens. We lend our money to the bank and the bank then loans money to local businesses or other borrowers. The bank pays us interest income and charges its borrowers a higher rate of interest. The bank tries to make a profit by collecting more than enough interest from its borrowers to pay all of its expenses. If the bank is successful in doing that, the net income will accrue to the owners of the bank who have bought common stock in the bank.

Most of us who put money in bank passbook accounts or CDs believe there is no risk of loss because the federal government guarantees or insures the safety of our deposits. Actually, it's not the government itself which insures the deposits. The Federal Deposit Insurance Corporation (FDIC) actually insures the deposits. The FDIC's income comes from fees it charges member banks. The federal government itself is not actually required to meet the obligations of the FDIC. Nevertheless, if the FDIC goes broke in guaranteeing deposits of bankrupt banks, the U.S. government will likely bail out the FDIC so it can meet its obligations. As the 1980s came to a close, the federal government did just that to a sister agency which failed. The Federal Savings and Loan Insurance Corp. (FSLIC) went broke and couldn't meet its obligations to guarantee deposits at failed savings and loan banks. So, the federal government bailed out the FSLIC.

Certainly, the FDIC insurance reduces the risk of loss for bank depositors. This lower risk usually means lower returns in the form of interest income. The period of the late 1970s and early 1980s was an exception to the general rule of low returns on CDs. The rate of interest on U.S. Treasury bills and bank CDs is closely related to the level of price inflation in consumer goods in the overall economy. In the late 1970s, inflation and interest rates shot up to historical high levels. For a brief time when interest rates peaked, CDs turned out to be excellent investments. However, that was then and this is now. Now and for the foreseeable future, CDs are not an ideal long-term investment because the interest rate on them is low in comparison to rates of return on some other investments. Additionally, as we saw in Chapter 3, if you want to make modest annual contributions to accumulate $1,000,000, you'll need a long period of years and a rate of return of 10% to 12% or better. CD rates don't do it!

When you compare CD interest rates to the level of inflation, you also come to the conclusion that the CD rates are low. Economists refer to the "real" rate of return. The "real" rate of return is the stated rate of return reduced by the rate of inflation. If a CD pays 5% interest and the rate of inflation is 4%, then the "real" rate of return is 1%. Gaining a net 1% annual compound rate of return in this hypothetical example is certainly a slow boat to China.

An investment very similar to the bank CD is the Guaranteed Investment Contract (GIC). The GIC is basically a CD sold by an insurance company. The GIC is often one of several choices for investors in 401(k) plans. The GIC is not insured by the FDIC. Its safety depends entirely on the financial solvency of the insurance company. As with CDs, the GICs typically pay too little in interest income to be the main holding in a young person's 401(k) plan. For investors who are within five or six years of retirement, they have some appeal due to their relatively low risk.

Government Securities

From a risk standpoint, U.S. Government securities are even better than FDIC insured bank CDs. They are direct obligations of the U.S. Treasury, backed by the "full faith and credit" of the federal government. Treasury bills have a short maturity (less than a year) and usually the lowest interest rates among U.S. Government securities. U.S. Treasury notes have an intermediate maturity (one to five years) and generally pay more interest than Treasury bills. Treasury bonds have long maturities and usually pay the most interest among Treasury securities. The higher yields on Treasury bonds come with a risk. It's called the interest rate risk. The interest rate risk could cause you to lose money on bonds, including Treasury bonds. Yes, that's right; you could lose money on U.S. Treasury bonds. (More on risk, including interest rate risk, later in this chapter.)

U.S. government agency securities are another type of government security. Undoubtedly, you've heard of some of these agencies. Examples include the Federal Housing Administration (FHA) and Tennessee Valley Authority (TVA). In addition to these government agencies, there are quasi-governmental agencies, such as Government National Mortgage Association (Ginnie Mae). These agencies and quasi-governmental agencies sell bonds to the public. The interest rate earned on agency bonds is generally slightly higher than the interest rate on direct Treasury bonds. Some of these agency bonds, for example Ginnie Mae securities, are backed by the full faith and credit of the U.S. Government. Most agency securities are not fully backed by the Treasury. Instead, Congress has the "moral obligation" to back them, if necessary.

Generally, U.S. Government and agency bonds are suitable only for the most conservative investors. Most investors will need higher rates of return to meet their long term goals.

One type of government security that is clearly unsuitable for IRA or 401(k) plans is the municipal government bond. The 50 states and other tax raising entities such as cities, school districts, public housing projects, etc. can issue municipal bonds to raise money. The interest income received by municipal bond investors is generally exempt from federal income taxes. Hence they're called tax-free investments. The tax-free benefit reduces the interest rate on these bonds. The low interest rate makes them a poor investment in any tax-deferred savings plan. Virtually no 401(k) plans offer them, and no prudent financial advisor would recommend them for an IRA.

Corporate Bonds

Corporate bonds are another type of creditor investment. The corporation borrows money from you, the investor, and gives you a corporate bond as evidence of the debt it owes you. The corporation then uses that money for its own profit making purposes, such as building a new factory. The corporation figures it can make a bit more money on its investment than it has to pay out in interest expense. The interest expense is fixed over the life of the bond, but the amount of income the corporation earns is flexible. Whether the corporation barely makes enough to pay its interest expense or makes many times more than the interest expense, the bond investor gets the fixed rate of interest. That fact is both the advantage and the disadvantage of the bond investment. The bond investors have the advantage of a stable return. In contrast, the owners of the corporation, the stockholders, have no assurance of getting any return at all. Therefore, the corporate bond is less risky than the corporate stock.

Since corporations do not have the power to tax anyone, the corporate bond is generally more risky than a government bond. As such, the corporate bond usually pays more interest income than does a government bond.

Intuitively, you know that some corporate bonds are less risky than others. Large well-established, highly profitable corporations are less risky than unprofitable corporations. Other corporate bonds with less risk are mortgage bonds. Mortgage or collateral bonds have tangible assets of the corporation backing up the bonds. Bonds that are not backed by tangible assets are called debenture bonds or debentures.

Historically, top rated bonds have been extremely safe. On the other hand, high-yield bonds, also called "junk bonds," are not so safe.

High-yield bonds were formerly issued by smaller companies that had to pay high yields to get some investors to buy them. It was expected that some of these companies might have a hard time meeting their interest expenses in time of recession. Thus, their bonds were low rated or non-rated by the bond rating services. In the 1980s, some larger, more established companies issued huge amounts of bonds to buy other companies. The total debt of the acquiring companies was so large in relation to their total assets that they had to pay high yields to accomplish their corporate takeover deals. When the economy slowed down in 1990, many of these companies were unable to make interest payments on their bonds.

There is quite a range in bond safety and bond yields. To make things easier for investors, there are rating services which give letter grades to bonds. For many years, Standard and Poor's ratings and Moody's ratings have been the industry standards. You can get the ratings books by subscription or you can find them in the business reference section of your public library. Rating services do not use crystal balls. Occasionally a bond may be highly rated up until the time of a drastic loss in the corporation's earnings. Overnight, the rating can drop several grades. Junk bonds are rated BB or lower, or get no rating at all.

Bond Ratings

Moody's	Standard & Poor's	Quality
Aaa	AAA	Highest quality
Aa	AA	High quality
A	A	Good quality
Baa	BBB	Medium quality
Ba	BB	Somewhat speculative
B	B	Speculative
Caa	CCC	Default possible
Ca	C	Default - partial recovery possible
C	D	Default - recovery not likely

The bond ratings grade the risk of default. Default occurs when the bond issuer is not able to pay the promised interest income or not able to pay back the principal at maturity.

There is another type of risk which applies to all bonds, including U.S. Government bonds. It's called interest rate risk. The interest rate risk is the risk that you'll have to sell bonds at a loss before they mature. At maturity, you'll get back the full principal amount of your investment. If you have to sell bonds before they mature, the market price may be more or less than 100% of the principal amount. If long-term interest rates go up after you

purchase bonds, the market value of the bonds will go down. On
the other hand, if long term interest rates go down, then your bonds
will go up in market value. Of course there are more types and
subtypes of debt securities than the ones described here. You can
contact an investment broker to learn more about other types of
bonds. A detailed description of these types of securities is beyond
the scope of this book.

As with bank CDs, there have been a few periods when bonds
have been outstanding investments for tax-deferred accounts.
Historically, in most periods, common stocks have done better than
CDs and bonds. While there's no guarantee that the past will repeat
itself, common stocks are expected to continue to outperform bonds
in the long term.

In summary, corporate bonds can be suitable for some investors.
Investors who buy bonds, particularly high-yield bonds, should
reduce their risks by *diversifying*. Diversifying means owning
several investments instead of one or two. There's more information
on diversifying later in this chapter.

Common Stocks

A common stock is partial ownership of a corporation. When a
corporation is formed, the owners contribute money or other assets
to the corporation. In return for those contributed assets, the
corporation issues shares of stock. Each share of stock is partial
ownership. The owners' contribution for each share of stock is
decided by the incorporators. Most corporations are closely held by
just one or a few people. In some cases the founders of the
corporation need more money to build factories, stores, etc. than
they are able to raise on their own. They can then get additional
capital either by borrowing money, or by selling more shares of
stock to other buyers who in turn become partial owners of the
corporation. By selling and issuing additional shares of stock, the
corporation becomes a publicly held corporation. While some large

corporations are closely held by a single family, most of the large corporations are publicly held.

Buying and selling. Many large companies regularly sell shares directly to the public. They also offer to reinvest dividends into additional shares of stock. However, most investors do not buy stock directly from the corporation. They buy previously owned shares from other investors. You buy pre-owned shares in the secondary market for stocks. If you want to buy stock in the secondary market, you can buy it directly from a current stock owner, or through a stockbroker. Most such purchases of common stocks are done through stockbrokers.

The secondary market got started in this country in 1792 when a small group of brokers starting meeting regularly under a tree near what is now Wall Street in New York City. Gradually, the system became more formalized, and the trading went indoors. About 2200 stocks are now traded at the New York Stock Exchange and about 1000 stocks are traded at the American Stock Exchange. The method of trading stock on both exchanges is the auction method. Stocks are sold to the highest bidder and purchased from the lowest offerer. Generally, when you want to buy or sell stocks, you place an order with a stockbroker. The local stockbroker is in touch with an associate on the floor of the exchange who executes the order through the specialist broker. Small orders are executed by computer at the current price. Some investors do their trading through brokers on the Internet.

There are many more stocks traded off the stock exchanges than on the exchanges. These stocks are commonly called over-the-counter (OTC) stocks. The National Association of Securities Dealers Automated Quotation System (NASDAQ) lists 3000 OTC stocks. If you want to buy or sell one of these stocks, your local broker will put in an order to a NASDAQ dealer, and the trade will be executed entirely by computer. If you're selling, you will automatically sell to the dealer offering the highest price among all the dealers making a market in that stock. Correspondingly, if you're buying, the computer will execute your trade with the dealer offering the lowest price on the NASDAQ system.

Some 11,000 smaller companies' stocks trade infrequently and therefore are not listed in the NASDAQ system. These stocks are not reported in the newspapers. You'll have to ask your broker to get pricing information from the so-called pink sheets.

Outstanding Opportunity. Since most of the large companies are publicly owned, investors have a wonderful opportunity to share in their success. As working people, our livelihoods revolve around a single employer which may not be growing and may not be making a lot of money. But as common stock investors, we have the opportunity for potentially unlimited financial growth. This outstanding potential is available not only to the founders of these corporations, but also to anyone who wants to buy common stock in these corporations through the secondary market.

By putting your money in bank CDs or GICs, you place a limit on how much you can earn. By putting your money in common stocks, you open yourself to unlimited opportunity for gains. Of course, once again, the risk is substantially greater in common stock than in CDs or GICs.

Hopefully, the company whose stock you own will make a profit, or have earnings. If so, it may keep all of its earnings to plow back into new factories, new stores, etc.; or it may pay out a portion of those earnings to shareholders. The portion of earnings distributed to shareholders is called dividends. Dividends are usually paid quarterly. The dividend yield is the amount of annual dividends divided by the price of the stock.

The total return on your common stock investment is the dividend yield plus or minus the percentage change in the value of the stock. Hopefully, your stock will go up in value. If so, you add the increase in the share price to the annual dividends to get total return. For example, if your stock paid $1 in annual dividends and increased in price during the year from $20 to $24 a share, your results would be as follows. Your dividend yield was $1 divided by $20 equal 5%. Your total gain was $1 dividend + $4 gain in share price or a total of $5. The $5 gain divided by $20 equals a 25% total return. If your stock declined in value from $20 to $17, your total loss would be $1 dividend minus $3 change in value or a total of $(2). The $2 loss divided by $20 equals a total return loss of 10%, which is expressed as (10%).

Typically, companies which keep most of their earnings have a low dividend yield. That money not paid out is called retained earnings. Hopefully, the retained earnings are used in such a way as to increase future earnings of the company. As future earnings per share of stock increase, the stock will tend to increase in value.

Companies which pay out most of their earnings in the form of dividends generally have a higher dividend yield. On the other hand, they tend to have less growth of future earnings and less gains in the values of their stocks.

Stocks are as different as people are

Some stocks you can pretty well count on to be around for a while. Others may be here today and gone tomorrow. The ones you can pretty well count on to be around are considered investment grade. The others are considered speculative. Within the investment grade category, there are several different types. Let's take a brief look at the major types.

Blue chip stocks are the largest and strongest companies, such as General Motors, IBM, General Electric, Johnson & Johnson, etc. These stocks have huge assets and huge earnings. They are well-established leaders in their particular industries. They are considered safe because they are unlikely to go bankrupt, even in tough economic times. They might have to reduce dividends in a bad recession and their stock prices may decline some, but they will most likely bounce back very well in better economic times.

Secondary stocks are smaller and not as well known, but they are established, successful, and relatively large companies. They are relatively safe, but certainly more risky than the blue chip stocks.

Income stocks are also large well-established companies. Their distinguishing characteristic is that they pay out a substantial portion of their earnings to shareholders in the form of dividends. They have a good historical record of stable dividend payments. Most successful utility stocks are in this category.

Growth stocks are companies which have shown very high growth in earnings per share of stock. These companies may be experiencing annual growth of 15%, 25%, 35%, or even more. Usually, they are smaller and newer companies, but not always. Some large, well established companies continue to achieve much higher than average growth. Dividends on growth stocks are usually low or nonexistent. These stocks are riskier than blue chip stocks because these companies may experience a quick and substantial drop in price per share of stock if the growth unexpectedly stops or slows down.

Cyclical stocks are companies which have relatively large earning increases in periods of prosperity, and large earning decreases in periods of recession. Companies in the automobile, steel, chemical, etc. industries tend to be cyclical. During the economic downturns, dividends may be cut, and investors start worrying about the possibility of bankruptcy. Thus, share prices tend to go down. During periods of prosperity, investors tend to believe that prosperity is here to stay or will last a very long time. Consequently, share prices tend to go up nicely when the economy is strong.

Defensive stocks have relatively stable earnings even during economic downturns. Food companies will continue to sell food because people have to eat even in times of recession. Utility companies are often both income stocks and defensive stocks. All of the above types of stocks are investment grade stocks.

Speculative stocks are more risky than investment grade stocks. These stocks are often new and small. They may have a history of negative earnings. Some may be barely meeting the interest payments on their debts. Others may be putting all their resources into an unproven product, or an unfinished oil well or a gold mine. Some speculative stocks sell for less than $1 per share. These are called *penny stocks*. For your important goals, you don't want to put your money into highly speculative stocks.

How to choose which stocks to buy

With so many types of stocks and so many stocks in each type, how do you know which stocks to buy? There are two methods to evaluate stocks. One is technical analysis and the other is fundamental analysis.

Technical analysis uses historical price changes and the related number of shares traded. The price changes are charted daily, weekly, or monthly. The historical information is used to predict future changes in a stock's price per share.

Fundamental analysis attempts to determine the fair or intrinsic value of a share of common stock. It is based on anticipated future earnings and dividends per share of stock. Fundamental analysis takes many things into account. It uses various financial ratios of the company's income statements and balance sheets. It uses historical percentage increases in earnings per share of common stock. It compares one company to another in the same industry. It compares one industry to another in terms of future outlook. Finally, it evaluates the human factors – how good is the company management. Fundamental analysis then puts all these factors together to ask: what is the estimated future earnings per share of stock, and what is a fair price to pay for the stock based on those earnings?

Emotions

We all like to think of ourselves as in control most of the time. We believe our behavior and decisions are rational and logical except in the few cases where we get really mad about something. Certainly, a decision to buy or sell a stock seems like a logical decision. We use technical analysis, fundamental analysis, or both to evaluate stocks. We study the numbers, hopefully, to make a good decision. Yet, easily the biggest danger facing stock investors is that their emotions may cause them to make poor buying and selling decisions.

When a substantial amount of your money is at stake, you will be emotionally involved. Every investor becomes emotionally involved. It's human nature. The problem is that your emotions could push you to make poor investment decisions. The hidden danger is not realizing how powerful these emotions are.

Greed for gain and fear of loss are the basic emotions of investing. Greed for gain is a strong desire to get rich quick. The way to get rich quick is to take huge risks. Generally, taking huge risks leads to disaster – the loss of much or all of the investment. Even professional investment analysts often take greater risks in their own portfolios than they do in the portfolios they manage for other people. A number of such investment professionals have related to me that although they get good results for their clients, they don't do so well for themselves. They can keep their emotions at bay when it's the other guy's money, but when it's their own money, emotions rule.

Following the crowd is one of the biggest emotional mistakes most investors make. When everybody is making money in the stock market, when your acquaintances are giving you stock tips, and when the professionals almost unanimously agree that the market will do nothing but go up and up, that's when the market is high and probably due for a drop. Almost everyone who has money to invest has already jumped on the bandwagon and bought all the stock they can afford. They have little or no new money to invest. Following the euphoria of the crowd in this situation tends to cause one to buy too high. The same principles apply when everybody knows that the stock market is a terribly risky money loser. The crowd has already sold their stocks and the market is probably near a bottom. Following the crowd here will result in selling too low. Few people have the fortitude to sell when everybody else is bullish; likewise, few people are willing to buy when everybody else is depressed from losses.

Ego

Making a mistake is a blow to your ego. Selling a stock at a loss is admitting that you made a mistake. So, if your stock goes down in price, it's human nature to hold on to the stock, hoping that it will go back up. After awhile, you say to yourself that "when the stock goes back up to what I paid for it, then I'll sell." That way you won't have to take a loss and admit the mistake of buying the stock in the first place. Too often in such a situation, the stock keeps going down and down and down. Most professionals will tell you to cut your losses by selling losing stocks quickly. To be very successful, you can't let your ego get in the way of making your decisions. As with greed and fear, the ego is very strong and usually wrong.

Stock brokers.

Stock brokers are first and foremost excellent sales people. Remember that a stock broker is generally a commissioned salesman. If the broker is on a salary, that salary is related to his or her volume of sales. The more you buy and sell, the more money the broker makes. The broker's income is unrelated to your profits or losses. Your broker will make a profit on your stock trading, even if you take a loss.

Most brokers are ethical, and they want you to do well in the stock market so you'll continue to do business with them. However, some brokers may recommend too much trading for your own good.

Stock tips

Relying on "hot tips" or second hand "inside information" can get you into trouble. First of all, it's almost a sure bet that the information you get has already been acted on by large buyers or sellers. It's like a chain letter. If you're not the first or second investor to act on the information, you won't get the goodies, so to speak.

Let's say the hot tip is that a small oil & gas company has just drilled a well which found huge reserves of oil. The company is keeping the success a secret for a short time. Now is the time to buy before the public announcement is made. Sounds like a great opportunity – almost too good to be true. It is too good to be true! If the facts are correct, other people have already acted on the information by buying as much stock as they could. All of that buying has already pushed up the price of the stock. By the time you get the tip, the stock has probably been run up about as much as it's going to. It may go a little higher after the announcement, but then the stock will probably drop due to profit taking. If the information is really publicly undisclosed inside information, you could be forced by the Securities & Exchange Commission to forfeit whatever gains you make from the inside information. Trading on inside information is against the law.

A much bigger danger is that the tip is false information or false rumors put out by insiders who want to sell their own shares at a high price. The real facts are a disaster. The company has drilled nothing but dry holes with its last reserves of cash. The company's stock will collapse as soon as the news is released. The insiders know this, and they want to sell their own shares before the stock drops. So, they start rumors that the oil wells look very promising. The rumor might be that a larger company strongly desires the assets of their company and will soon offer to pay far more than the stock is currently trading for. Once again, you weren't the first to get the information. If the information is true, the stock has already gone up. If the information is false, there will be a high volume of trading with little or no upward price movement. For every buyer, there is a seller. The sellers are insiders who know that the real facts are a disaster. The selling pressure of the insiders prevents the stock from moving up sharply. Does this kind of thing happen often? I don't believe so, but it does happen. I'm well acquainted with a very bright, well-educated man who got such a tip from his "friends." With too much trust in the greedy tipsters and too much greed on his own part, he lost his life savings.

Online and printed information

I refer to both Internet information and standard printed information as printed information. Your computer "prints" the Internet information on your computer screen. Of course you want printed information about stocks you're interested in. But once again, others have already gotten and acted on that information before you get a chance to see it, either in print or on the Internet. Realize that if your broker has a good idea, he's already shared the idea with larger customers. If the home office of a brokerage firm puts out a written report on a stock, the home office analysts have already verbally told the story to their largest institutional customers. That's just how it works. So, you've got two problems. One is that you're playing against professional, full-time money managers. The other problem is that they are probably getting information before you do.

There's another problem with printed information. Everything you read is not necessarily true. According to public, printed information, two major Canadian gold mining companies found very big discoveries of gold, one in Nevada and another in Indonesia. In 1997, the companies admitted that the rock samples were tampered with and prior reports were false. Many investors, including some institutional investors, lost millions of dollars in these two fiascos because they had relied on companies' original reports.

No diversification

No matter how large, how reputable, how popular a company is, it is too risky to put all your savings into the stocks of just one or two companies. The old adage "don't put all your eggs in one basket" is appropriate for stock investments, as well as bond investments.

To protect yourself from the risk of your favorite one or two stocks going belly up, you need to own twenty to a hundred stocks. If you think the stocks of retail stores are a good investment, don't just buy one or two of them. Diversify geographically. Retail stores generally serve regional areas rather than the whole country. Therefore, buy stock in stores which serve more than one region. If one region suffers a recession, the other region or regions may have a much better economy. Of course, you could be wrong about retail stocks. A very poor Christmas season could bankrupt some retail companies. Own stocks in more than one industry. High tech could be good. Perhaps computers. Computer stocks have done well and may continue to do so. However, if computer companies build too many factories and can't sell all their computers, prices will drop, profits may drop and the companies could do poorly. The value of your computer investments could go down sharply.

So you continue to diversity into more stocks in additional industries. If you own good stocks in several industries, a few stocks could do poorly, while good performance in other stocks would prevent bad overall results. The good performance in the rest of the portfolio could more than offset the losses and produce favorable net returns.

What if the economy went into a severe recession or depression? Wouldn't all stocks do poorly, thus negating the benefits of diversification? Not necessarily! People still have to eat. Good companies could stay healthy. Companies that make replacement parts for used cars could do better than normal as consumers keep their old cars longer. Some companies are international in scope. A decline in sales in one country, such as the U.S., could be offset by gains in other regions of the world. Additionally, you could own some foreign stocks as part of the diversification plan.

Although diversification doesn't eliminate risk of loss, it does substantially reduce the risk. Of course, diversification also reduces the possibility of huge gains.

It's too ridiculous. Yes, the stock market has potential, but how are you going to pick your stocks? There are risks of relying totally on brokers or friends with tips. Printed financial information available to you is outdated by the time you get it. You don't have the time to research the stock market to select the needed 20 to 100 stocks for good diversification. Once you decide on your investment choices, you have the huge problem of dealing with your own emotions and ego. Therefore, for most people, it's not a good idea to do your own stock picking for your most important goals. If you have extra money to play with or speculate with, then buy individual stocks. However, for your retirement money, the best solution to the problems discussed above is mutual funds. Investing in mutual funds is the best investment strategy for most long-term investors.

CHAPTER 8

HIGHLIGHTS OF MUTUAL FUNDS

Introduction to Mutual Funds

The very first mutual fund was started in 1924 in Boston. Since that time, the popularity of mutual funds has skyrocketed. Most of the growth has occurred in recent years. In 1990 fund assets totaled one trillion dollars and by 1993 the total doubled to more than two trillion. By 1994, there were more than 5300 mutual funds of all categories in the U.S. There are now more than 6000 stock funds.

The mutual fund industry has contributed substantially both to individual fund investors and the general economy. For example, bond funds specializing in mortgage backed securities have expanded the market for mortgage loans. The result has been more mortgages available to U.S. homeowners at lower rates of interest. Thus, mutual funds have made it easier for millions of Americans to own their own homes.

Mutual fund growth has also contributed to the number of jobs available in the economy. Many aggressive mutual funds buy initial public offerings (IPO) of stock in young, small companies. The money invested in these small companies allows them to grow and create millions of new jobs. Mutual funds which don't buy IPOs also contribute to the economy. They buy the stocks of these small companies after they have become larger and more successful. They may buy subsequent public offerings of additional shares in these growing companies, thus allowing the companies to continue to grow rapidly. The funds may buy stock from other investors who previously

101

bought the stock directly from issuing companies. In this more typical case, buying stock from other investors, the benefit to the economy is indirect, but substantial. The purchasers of IPOs would not invest nearly as much as they do without knowing that there is a large secondary market for these stocks.

Of course there would be home mortgages and IPOs of small companies without the existence of mutual funds. The point is that mutual funds have made these markets bigger and better.

Millions of investors know they don't have the expertise to pick their own stocks. As such, these investors do not risk money in the stock market. Yet they do put substantial money in the stock market indirectly by purchasing mutual funds.

The mutual fund industry has provided great wealth to the individual investors in the funds. The funds have enabled many investors to earn higher rates of return on their fund investments than they would have earned outside of the funds.

What is a Mutual Fund?

A mutual fund is a corporation whose sole purpose is to invest the money of its shareholders, generally into stocks, bonds, money market instruments, or a combination of these investments. Like any corporation, a mutual fund sells its own shares to investors who become shareholders in the mutual fund. The mutual fund "pools" money from its shareholders and invests it according to a shared or "mutual" objective. The fund attempts to do a better job of investment management for its shareholders than the shareholders could do on their own.

Each fund has its own objective or combination of objectives, as stated in the fund's prospectus. The three major objectives of any investment, including mutual funds are as follows:

1) stability of principal – protection from loss.
2) growth – increasing the value of the principal.
3) income – a stream of earnings paid out to the investors.

There are numerous ways that mutual funds attempt to reach their goals. Some funds are aggressive and take high risks; others are very conservative and avoid risks as best they can. Different funds use a range of tactics or policies to meet their objectives. These policies are also stated in the funds' prospectuses. Each fund manager takes into account the fund's objectives and policies when choosing investments for that fund. Likewise, potential investors consider a fund's objectives and policies when choosing a fund to invest in.

The mutual fund receives dividends from stocks held in its portfolio, and it also receives interest income on its holdings of bonds or other debt investments. After deductions of fund expenses, the fund pays out all of its earnings to its shareholders in the form of *dividends*. In addition, the fund pays out earnings generated from portfolio securities sold at a profit. These earnings are called *capital gains distributions*. Dividends and capital gains are paid out in proportion to the number of shares owned. Thus, shareholders who only own a few shares get the same investment return per dollar invested as those who invest hundreds of thousands of dollars. Increases or decreases in the value of the fund's investment portfolio are reflected in the net asset value per share (NAV) of the fund.

Unlike regular corporations, there is no double taxation of income. The mutual fund pays no income taxes on its earnings. Mutual funds are not allowed to accumulate earnings from one year to the next. All dividend and interest income is paid out to shareholders during the year. Likewise, all net short-term and long-term capital gains are paid out to shareholders by year-end. Shareholders can take these payments either in cash or in additional shares. If taken in additional shares, the number of additional shares is based on the net asset value per share at the time of the distribution. The reinvestment of dividends is considered a cash distribution plus an immediate "cash" investment into the additional shares.

How Funds Operate

The shareholders of a mutual fund own the fund. All shares issued by a mutual fund must have equal voting rights. The shareholders elect a board of directors to oversee the management of the fund. The board of directors hires officers to manage the day-to-day operations of the fund, or it hires a management company to do this job. The management company is not owned by the shareholders of the mutual fund. It works for the mutual fund.

The management company is usually the organization which created the fund, and generally serves as the fund's investment adviser. As such, it has on staff investment analysts and portfolio managers who buy and sell securities for the fund.

The fund may also contract with a custodian, an underwriter, and a transfer agent. The custodian is usually a bank. The custodian pays for securities purchased, receives payments when investments are sold, and holds and safeguards the portfolio of securities.

The underwriter handles the sale of fund shares to the public. It may act as a retailer or as a wholesaler of fund shares to retail brokers.

The transfer agent performs all of the record keeping services for the fund's shareholders. It records transactions in each shareholder account and it pays out dividends and capital gains distributions.

The management company charges the fund a management fee based on the total net assets of the fund. The fund also pays its other operating expenses. These expenses include charges for custodian fees, transfer agent fees, printing, postage, accounting and legal fees. It is expensive; however, due to the large size of the typical mutual fund's assets, the total operating expense as a percentage of assets are generally quite low. In many cases, the total is not much more than 1.0%. In some cases, the total is less than 1.0%.

Buying and Selling Mutual Funds

On each day the financial markets are open for trading, the fund calculates its net asset value per share (NAV). A *no-load fund* sells new shares and redeems or buys back shares at the NAV. To calculate the NAV, the fund uses the day's closing market price of each holding in the fund. It adds the total value of the portfolio holdings to its other assets (cash and receivables) and subtracts accrued expenses and liabilities. That total of net assets is divided by the number of shares outstanding to get the net asset value per share – NAV. In the standard *load fund*, shares are purchased at the offering price, which is the NAV plus a sales charge.

A no-load fund sells its own shares directly to investors at NAV. A *low-load fund* sells its own shares directly to investors with a low, usually 2% or 3% sales load, added on.

A load fund pays a sales commission to the broker, agent, or planner who sells the fund's shares. Of course, there's no free lunch. The investor pays an additional amount in order for the salesman to receive a commission. Several years ago, that additional amount was always easy to identify. It was a percentage of NAV added to the sales price. It's more complicated now. Although the additional amount, or load, generally goes to a maximum of 6.5%, it can go as high as 8.5%. Once your account value reaches certain levels, the load percentage usually drops substantially. On very large accounts, it may go down to 1.0% or even less. This type of fund which adds a sales charge to NAV at purchase is called a *front-end load fund*.

Many fund investors like to buy funds through brokers, but they don't like the high front-end loads. Therefore, the industry has developed ways to compensate the salesperson without charging the investor a high front-end load. Some funds accomplish this by charging either a *back-end load* or a redemption fee. In most cases, the back-end load disappears gradually over a period of time, usually six years. The back end load is also called a *contingent deferred sales charge*. If the investor holds the fund for less than the six years, the investor pays a sales load upon sale (redemption) of the shares. If the holding period is more than the six years, there's no load at redemption. However, in these back-end load funds, there is an additional annual distribution fee. That annual fee is called the

Rule 12b-1 fee. Rule 12b-1 of the Investment Company Act of 1940 allows this fee, which is usually 1.00% each year for load funds.

Any mutual fund can charge a 12b-1 fee. Even a "no-load" fund can charge a 12b-1 fee of up to .25%. So, you can't totally rely on the description of "no-load" to be assured that there are no sales or distribution charges. To check out fees and other policies of a fund, you can read the fund's prospectus, or you could ask the agent or broker about sales loads and 12b-1 fees.

Sales loads are neither good nor bad. If you have a knowledgeable broker who provides fund selection or financial planning services for you, then the load compensates the broker for value added to you. If you don't need these services from a broker, then you are better off to buy a true no-load fund without a 12b-1 fee. Most no load funds have toll-free telephone numbers which can be found in various trade publications, such as the quarterly issue of "The Wall Street Journal."

The above information pertains to *open-end mutual funds*. Open-end mutual funds sell and redeem (buy back) shares every day that the New York Stock Exchange is open. The other type of mutual fund is the *closed-end fund*. Closed-end funds sell shares when the fund is new, and do not redeem their shares. Since most mutual funds are open-end, this book relates only to open-end funds.

All new investors of load or no-load funds must be furnished with a prospectus of the fund at or prior to the time of investment. The prospectus is the fund's official document of important information. The prospectus describes the fund's investment objectives, policies, services, management, sales charges (if any), historical performance, and expenses. A Statement of Additional Information (SAI) may also be requested by the investor.

Federal Regulation

The mutual fund industry is highly regulated, mostly by the federal Securities & Exchange Commission (SEC). The SEC administers several laws, but the two most important are the

Securities Act of 1933 and the Investment Company Act of 1940. The Securities Act of 1933 basically requires that the fund must furnish full and complete disclosure of financial and other corporate information to potential investors in the fund's prospectus. This information provides investors with the necessary facts on which to make an informed investment decision. The SEC reviews the information and allows the fund to sell its shares only after it is satisfied that no important information has been left out. The SEC's approval of the prospectus is in no way an endorsement of the fund. The SEC's approval is merely its opinion that full disclosure has been made. If it turns out that the fund has not made full disclosure according to the law, the law allows shareholders to sue the fund. Of course, if this problem occurs, it will be handled as a class action suit. Individual shareholders will not have to go to the time and expense of getting their own lawyers.

The Investment Company Act of 1940 (ICA) requires a minimum level of securities diversification in diversified mutual funds. It also has numerous other provisions. It restricts conflicts of interest and transactions between the fund and its officers. It provides for the safekeeping of fund assets. Fund assets are held by an independent custodian, generally a bank. Insurance in the form of a fidelity bond is required to ensure against theft. The SEC specifies that each fund must have a certain percentage of board directors who are independent of the fund's adviser or underwriter.

Professional Management

Generally, the professional investment manager can do a better job for you than you can do for yourself. There are several reasons the professional manager is able to get better performance. One reason is that he or she experiences less emotional pressure. High emotional pressure often results in poor investment decisions, and the emotional pressure of managing someone else's money is far less than the pressure of managing your own money.

The mutual fund management company has full-time professionals to manage the fund's investments. It stands to reason that full-time managers will do better than part-time managers. Some investment professionals who work outside of mutual funds are not full time investment managers. They work full time, but spend only part-time in managing client investments. Generally, retail stockbrokers spend most of their time on the telephone with current or prospective customers. With investment advisory firms, the professionals responsible for managing investments may spend up to 40 percent of their time with clients and potential clients. Thus, these people are both investment managers and marketing managers.

The mutual fund manager, by contrast, is strictly an investment manager. Most fund managers do not speak to shareholders or potential shareholders of the fund. And if they do, it's very limited. The investment manager is judged by one thing – his or her investment performance. Other mutual fund personnel perform the marketing and servicing functions. If you have a question or problem and call to talk to the portfolio manager about it, you will get a shareholder service representative instead. If you write a letter to the portfolio manager, your letter will go to a customer relations representative for reply. If you need any personal attention, you'll have to get it from someone other than the portfolio manager.

A full time investment manager is insulated from the greed, fear, and other emotions of the shareholders. That's good for the shareholders. Talking to shareholders about investments would not only take up valuable time, but it would also put pressure on the manager to go against his or her own expert opinion. After all, it's hard to resist the suggestions of those who pay you. If the portfolio manager were under heavy client pressure to sell one of the fund's stocks, the manager would probably do so to get the clients off his or her back, so to speak. The fact is that the professional knows more about the merits of the stock than the clients do.

Mutual fund investment managers are extremely well paid. A good manager has no problem in getting a substantial six figure salary.

That's another advantage of investing in mutual funds. Mutual funds pay what it takes to get the managers they want.

Some mutual funds are managed by a group of portfolio managers (the committee system), while other funds are managed by a single manager (the star system). You'll be able to find out what system a particular fund uses by calling the fund, reading the prospectus, or reviewing a monitoring service such as Morningstar or Value Line. If the star leaves the fund, that information will also be printed in the monitoring services.

It is important to note that even in the star system, a portfolio manager is generally not on his or her own entirely. Typically, the investment management company employs a supporting research staff to assist the portfolio manager. The research staff performs extensive economic and financial analysis on the overall economy, various industries in the economy, and particular stocks in each industry. Both staff and portfolio manager read widely. They read general business publications, trade publications and research reports sent by brokerage firms and other sources. They study financial statements and make estimates of the future financial performance of individual stocks. They even talk to executives in the companies whose stocks they are interested in.

Although, I keep referring to mutual fund investments as stocks, a mutual fund may also own bonds and money market investments, including U.S. Treasury securities. The types of investments a fund owns depend on its investment objective.

Diversification

Diversification is a proven method of reducing investment risks. Therefore, diversification is absolutely basic as an investment principle for mutual funds. Diversification can take several different forms.

1. A number of different securities issuers. The Investment Company Act of 1940 sets minimum standards that a fund must meet to qualify as a diversified fund. Also, the Internal Revenue Code requires a fund to meet diversification standards in order to qualify as a regulated investment company.

2. A number of different industries in the portfolio. Most common stock funds diversify their portfolios by including stocks in many different industries. Most corporate bond funds and balanced funds do the same. However, a mutual fund could meet the minimum legal requirements of diversification by investing in only one industry. Funds that invest in a single industry are called *sector funds*. Such funds may limit their investments to bank stocks or insurance company stocks or gold mining stocks, etc. Even outside a sector fund, a mutual fund may concentrate a significant portion of its investments in one or two industries. Any fund that intends to invest 25% or more of its assets in a single industry must disclose that fact in its prospectus. Funds which don't have broad diversification in many different industries are more risky than other funds. Their performance tends to be quite volatile, up strongly in some years and down sharply in other years.

3. A number of different asset types in the portfolio. Rather than owning only stocks or only bonds, some funds own both stocks and bonds. These funds are called *balanced funds*. Funds with the greatest degree of diversification may own a combination of U.S. stocks, international stocks, U.S. bonds, international bonds, gold stocks, real estate stocks, and money market assets such as certificates of deposit (CDs). Few funds are as fully diversified as the above example. Most investors don't want or need that much diversification. Most of the investors who do want that degree of diversification own more than one fund.

The importance of diversification in reducing risk cannot be overstated. Too many people lose their life savings by putting all their money into a single stock or a single bond. It pays a high return and the broker or salesperson assures them that it's perfectly safe. If it were as safe as they believe, the investment return wouldn't be so high. It is unfortunate that so many people don't understand the high risk of a single stock or bond. You can dramatically reduce risks and still get a good investment return by investing in well diversified mutual funds.

Mutual Fund Services

The mutual fund industry is very competitive. Funds want your money, and they make it easy to do business with them. Consequently, they offer some very beneficial services to the customer or shareholder.

Detailed Record keeping. You'll receive a confirmation statement each time you purchase or sell shares in the fund and each time the fund makes a distribution to you. Annually, the fund will send you a cumulative statement showing all transactions for the year as well as the total number of shares in your account.

Telephone service. Most funds have toll-free telephone numbers. If you have a question about the fund or your account, you can talk to a customer service representative at no charge.

Exchange privilege. If your fund is part of a "family of funds" (a group of funds managed by the same company), you have great flexibility in exchanging money from one fund to another one. Just write the fund with your instructions for exchange. The transfer agent for the fund family will make the exchange and send you a confirmation notice in the mail. Some funds execute exchanges with no transaction fee to the shareholder. Some funds charge $5 for each exchange, and some funds limit the number of exchanges you can make in a year's time. The prospectus provides all the information you need to know about exchanges. You can call the fund's toll-free number to ask about these fees.

Telephone exchange & redemption. In many fund groups you can make fund exchanges or redemptions by telephone. This service has to be authorized by you in advance, usually on the initial account application.

Automatic investment. You can have your checking account automatically drafted each month to purchase fund shares. In most retirement account arrangements, such as a 401(k) plan, your employer will make your contributions directly from payroll deduction.

Automatic reinvestment. You can request to receive income and capital gains distributions either in cash or in additional shares of the fund. With tax-deferred retirement accounts, you will want distributions to be reinvested. Prior to age 59½, any cash distributions to you from a tax-deferred retirement account are subject to penalty income taxes.

Wire transfers. You can purchase or redeem shares through bank wire for increased speed. Wire transfers are made directly between the mutual fund's bank (custodian) and your bank. Your bank will certainly charge for this service, and the fund company might also impose a small fee.

Automatic withdrawal plans. These plans allow periodic redemptions of a specific dollar amount from the fund. Usually, the fund requires that the account size be at least $5,000 or $10,000 and the payment amount be at least $50 or $100 per month. These plans are popular with retirees who are no longer making contributions into their retirement accounts.

Rights of accumulation. This feature can lower the sales charge for front-end load funds. Typically with front-end load funds, the sales charge, which is a percentage of the amount invested, declines at several "break points." For instance, the percentage of sales charge might start at 6.5% and then drop to 5.0% at $25,000 and drop again at the $50,000+ level. Right of accumulation takes into account your total holdings in all funds in the fund family when applying the sales charge to new investments. Of course, no-load funds don't have this feature because they have no sales charges.

Letter of intent. Once again, this applies only to load funds. An investor can pay the lower percentage of sales charges if he or she signs a letter promising to make additional investments to reach the break point within 13 months. If the customer does not reach the breakpoint within 13 months, the account will be assessed the additional sales charge due.

Mutual Fund Advantages

Easy to monitor. Mutual funds calculate their results on a daily basis. You can find out how your fund is doing by going to the business-financial section of your daily newspaper or "The Wall Street Journal." It's easy to read the mutual funds section of a daily newspaper. Mutual funds are covered in their own table near the back of the business section in most local papers. Some daily newspapers report different information on the funds each day. For instance, on Mondays the paper may note which funds have a sales charge and which are no-load. On Tuesdays, the paper may provide price change in NAV from the day before. On Wednesdays, the paper may provide performance data for the last 12 months, etc. Of course, the newspaper has a box with explanations within the mutual funds table.

Whatever performance figures are listed in the newspaper, the assumption is that dividends and distributions have been reinvested into additional shares of the fund. Also, performance figures do not take into account sales loads or redemption fees.

Don't think you should check your holdings every day in the newspaper. Quarterly or annually is fine. If you have to check the value of your investments every day, and you worry every day when the price is down, then you probably should not be in a stock fund.

Other financial publications, magazines, and services report fund performance results for various time periods. Most likely you'll find CDA Weisenberger Investment Services, Value Line Mutual Funds or Morningstar Mutual Funds at your library. These three services provide continuous monitoring and rating reports on mutual funds. At first glance, their reports look very intimidating, with all the tables of numbers. However, I think you'll find these reports to be much easier to work with after seeing them two or three times. Additional periodicals which cover mutual funds include: Money, Forbes, Fortune, and Barron's. Certainly, there are many more publications which are also very good.

Flexible. As noted previously, mutual funds offer a number of services allowing you to buy, redeem, and exchange shares easily and quickly. The price you pay or receive for your shares is based on the net asset value calculated after receipt of the order. If your order is received before the daily close of the New York Stock Exchange, the price will be calculated as of the close on that day. If the order is received after the market closes, your price will be the next business day's price. This is called *forward pricing.*

Available. Most mutual funds have toll-free telephone numbers, which are included in the reports of the rating services listed above. What about minimum investment requirements? A few funds are closed to new investors. Some funds require a minimum investment of $5000 or more. However, most funds are readily available to the general public and have a minimum investment of $500 or less. There are some funds with a minimum of only $1.00.

Takes little time. That's important because you probably don't have the time to do much more than read this book. Chapter 11 covers how to select a suitable fund for you. That research can be done fairly quickly. Once that's done, all you really need to do is monitor the progress of your fund(s) quarterly or annually.

Low costs. The costs of mutual fund ownership are very reasonable and very clearly stated in the fund's prospectus. Every fund prospectus is required to have a detailed table of fund expenses. Table 8-1 shows an example of what this section of the prospectus is like.

Table 8-1
Fund Expenses

Shareholder Transaction Expenses:	
Sales charge on purchases	6.5%
Sales charge on reinvested dividends	-0-
Redemption fees	-0-
Exchange fees	$5.00 per exchange
Annual Fund Operating Expenses:	
Management fees	0.65%
12b-1 distribution fees	None
Other operating expenses	0.26%
Total operating expenses	0.91%

No-load funds charge nothing for sales and redemptions, but may charge up to .25% for 12b-1 fees. The front-end load fund in the above example charges 6.5% on fund purchases. A load of almost any amount is high if the fund is held only one year. In the above example, a 6.5% load on a $1000 investment amounts to $65 in the first year. But spread over ten years, the cost is $6.50 per year.

Annual fund operating expenses are less than 1.5% for the majority of common stock funds. Annual fund operating expenses for bond funds are usually less than 1.0%. The operating expenses listed in the prospectus reflect the actual expenses for the most recent year. Future expenses could increase or decrease from those stated in the prospectus; however, these expenses are usually quite stable.

Of course, what you want is a high net investment return in relation to the risks of your investment. The net return is gross return minus expenses. Generally speaking, both operating expenses and net returns increase as risk increases.

Reading Fund Literature

Reading the prospectus
The prospectus is a legal document, and as such, has some technical information that average investors may not fully understand. Don't be afraid to ask your stockbroker or financial planner for help in understanding its provisions; or feel free to call the toll-free number of the fund, whether the fund is load or no-load.

When I read a prospectus, I don't read it from cover to cover. I look at what I believe are the most critical parts first. The very first thing to look at is the date on the cover of the prospectus. Prospectuses must be updated no later than 16 months after the fund's last fiscal year end. Most are updated at least annually. Be sure you are reading the most recent edition.

Logically, the next thing to check is the minimum dollar amount required to open an account. If the amount is too high for you, trash the prospectus. From a more practical standpoint, I would simply ask the broker what the minimum is before even getting a prospectus. If the fund is no load, I would call the fund and ask the fund representative what the minimum is before asking the representative to send me a prospectus.

Fund expenses are covered at the beginning of the prospectus. An example of this section was covered previously in Table 8-1. Other important information may be disclosed several pages into the prospectus.

The section on investment objectives provides a rather broad description of the portfolio manager's philosophy. Be sure your objectives match the objectives of the fund. For example, if your objective is preservation of principal or a steady stream of income, then you don't want the fund's stated objective to be capital appreciation, and vice-versa.

The section on investment practices and restrictions provides more detailed information about what the fund can do with your money. On the one hand, you don't want the portfolio manager to be so tied down with restrictions that he or she can't take advantage of good opportunities. On the other hand, if you want to avoid an extremely high risk fund, there are some things the fund should not be allowed to do. The fund's prospectus should not say anything about buying commodities or energy exploration projects. If it does, consider that fund too speculative. Another very speculative investment policy is "short selling." Short selling is borrowing stock and then selling that stock. An exception to the above is "short selling against the box," a technical term which need not concern you. Short selling against the box is not a risky procedure. A less speculative but still high risk procedure is margin buying. Margin buying is borrowing money in order to buy investments. If a fund's prospectus states that the fund will engage in any of the above procedures, I recommend avoiding that fund as overly risky.

In my view, one of the most important items in the prospectus is found in the "Financial Highlights" section. That section provides the historical performance for one share of the fund. In that section you'll see a table of numbers that might cause you to reach for a headache remedy! No need. Simply look for the line TOTAL RETURN, usually in the middle of the chart. That line shows the total performance (income + capital gains or losses + change in the value of the fund) for each year over the last 10 years. Some years will probably show a loss, while other years show a gain. This table shows how good the best years have been and how bad it has been in the worst years.

Be sure to keep a copy of the prospectus in your files. You'll want to refer to the section on How to Redeem Shares when you're ready to sell. You may also want to refer to the section on exchanges from one fund into another fund within the same family of funds.

Reading your fund's annual and semiannual reports

The annual and semiannual reports are much more reader friendly than the prospectus. They are also quite informative. At the beginning of each report there is a letter from the fund's president to the fund's shareholders. This letter is worth reading. Typically, the president will review the overall economy, securities markets, and performance of the fund since the last report. The letter will usually explain why and what the fund did since the last report and give an outlook for the future. The letter provides more of a personal "feel" of the philosophy and strategy of the fund's management than does the legalistic prospectus.

Additionally, the report lists each investment in the fund's portfolio. It's not necessary to study the portfolio, but it is helpful to briefly review the names of the securities and the industries represented. Do you recognize any of the companies in the portfolio? Do you have an opinion of these companies? If you're a conservative investor and if you don't recognize any of the companies, perhaps this fund is not for you. You may want to see the names of large, well-established companies in the portfolio. You will also want to see fairly wide diversification among several different industries. You don't want 50% of the portfolio in just three industries. If you're more of a risk taker, you won't mind seeing names of companies you've never heard of and some concentration in a few industries. In fact, that may be exactly what you want.

Reading your fund's statements

Your mutual fund statement shows your most recent transaction or all of your transactions since the preceding December 31. While each fund has its own particular statement, the one shown in Table 8-2 is approximately what your fund's statement will look like.

Table 8-2 Mutual Fund Statement

ABC Mutual Fund, Inc.	John Doe
P.O. Box 1234	1234 Anywhere Lane
Money City, State 45678	Fair City, State 12345

1-800-123-4567

		Fund No.	Account No.
		23	11122233

Confirm Date	Trade Date	Transaction	Dollar Amount	Share Price	Shares This Transaction	Shares Owned
		Beg. Balance				0.000
01/06	01/02	Purchase	2000.00	18.20	109.890	109.890
01/29	01/26	Income Reinv. $.30	32.97	18.25	1.807	111.697
04/01	03/28	Purchase	1000.00	18.38	54.407	166.104
06/30	06/30	Service Fee	-10.00	18.40	-0.543	165.561

The statement starts with the name and address of the fund and then the name and address of the account owner (yourself). Near the top of the statement is your account number. Of course, in any correspondence with the fund, you'll want to reference your account number. The seven columns state the following information.

Confirm Date. On this date the fund recorded the transaction.

Trade Date. On this date the transaction actually occurred. The transaction will reflect the net asset value (NAV) as of this date. This date may differ from the confirm date. If it does, just ignore the confirm date.

Transaction. This column provides a brief description of what happened in your account. If you bought shares, it will say Purchase.

In that case you created the transaction and you'll be expecting to receive a confirmation from the fund within a couple of weeks. In some other cases, the fund will make transactions in your account. The fund makes transactions to redeem shares to cover the annual service charge on IRA accounts. Additionally, each time the fund makes distributions of dividends or capital gains, it will be recorded as a transaction. In Table 8-2, the second transaction shows that a distribution of $.30 per share has been reinvested into additional shares in the account.

Dollar Amount. This is the dollar amount of the transaction. In the above example, the distribution was $0.30 times the number of shares of the fund owned just before the distribution. $0.30 times 109.890 shares equals $32.97 in dollars.

Share Price. This is the fund price per share on the trade date. For no-load funds, it is the NAV. For load funds, the share prices include the sales charge for new purchases. Very few load funds charge a sales load on reinvested distributions.

Shares this Transaction. This is the number of shares purchased or redeemed in the transaction. It is computed by dividing the dollar amount by the share price.

Total shares owned. This is your ending cumulative number of shares owned after the transaction.

Fund Categories

The basic fund categories are money market funds, bond funds, stock funds, combination funds, and specialty funds. Within each basic category, there are several subcategories.

Money market funds

Money market funds invest in money market investments. These investments include U.S. Treasury bills, certificates of deposit, commercial paper, and other similar short-term debt. The investment objective is capital preservation with some current income. They are considered the safest mutual funds because the underlying securities (Treasury bill, CDs, etc.) are short-term, and the underlying securities generally have very little credit risk. These funds generally have a constant net asset value (NAV) of $1.00 per share. The major subcategories are taxable money market funds and tax-exempt money market funds.

Money market funds are appropriate where the investors' goals are short-term (less than five years). Generally, these funds provide the lowest investment return.

Bond funds

By definition, bond funds invest in bonds. In order of importance the objectives of bond funds are income, capital preservation, and capital appreciation. Bond funds can and do go up and down in value. The major subcategories are municipal bond funds, government income funds, corporate bond funds, and high-yield bond funds.

Municipal bond funds invest in bonds issued by governments below the federal level. The income from these state and local bonds is exempt from federal income tax. Mutual fund dividends are tax-exempt to the extent that the fund's earnings come from municipal bond interest income.

U.S. Government funds own a variety of bonds and notes issued by the U.S. federal government or government agencies. Some government funds own government insured mortgages. These funds are not guaranteed by the federal government. Their principal values will increase when interest rates decline, and principal values will decrease when interest rates go up. Because of the interest rate risk, these funds are not totally safe. All bond funds are subject to interest rate risk. Additionally, all mutual funds are subject to purchasing power risk.

Corporate bond funds seek a higher level of income than government bond funds provide. The risk is greater; so the return needs to be greater. These funds invest most of their assets in corporate bonds. A small portion of assets may be invested in money market instruments. Long-term bond funds will have a greater change in value as interest rates rise and fall. Short-term funds will fluctuate the least. Most of the corporate bond funds invest in high grade bonds with little credit risk. The funds which invest in low grade bonds have their own category. This category is usually called *high-yield bond funds* or *junk bond funds.*

High-yield bond funds invest mostly in corporate bonds rated Ba or lower by Moody's and BB or lower by Standard & Poor's rating services. Because these bonds are lower grades, they will have higher yields than investment grade corporate bonds. But don't assume that because the risk is quite a bit greater that the yield will also be substantially greater. The spread in yields between high-yield bonds and high grade bonds may be very small. High-yield bond funds tend to be the most volatile of all the bond funds. There are two reasons for this volatility. First, the bond maturities are typically long-term, which subjects them to the greatest interest rate risk. Second, the spread in yields between high yield bonds and high grade bonds may vary from less than 1.00% to more than 4.00%.

Stock Funds

Stock funds seek current income, capital appreciation, or both through investments in common stocks. Portfolio managers follow different styles in selecting stocks for their mutual funds. The two major styles are value and growth.

Value style

Value managers seek to buy stocks at a price below what they are intrinsically worth. The idea is that eventually the market will recognize what a bargain a particular stock is. At that time, the stock will attract enough buyers to bid the price of the stock up to what it is intrinsically worth. These managers follow textbook techniques for determining the fair value of a stock. They look at the price-earnings ratio, the dividend yield, and the price to book value ratio. They also look for values not reflected in the company's statement of assets and liabilities. Such values may be in real estate listed on the books at cost but worth far more. Other values may include newly discovered oil fields or patents on new products.

One major reason that some stocks sell below what appears to be their intrinsic worth is that the stocks have received bad publicity. The bad publicity is usually a recent drop in earnings, a drop in the rate of earnings growth, or a prediction of future such declines. Such bad news may trigger an over reaction on the part of investors. They may ignore the long-term prospects of the stock and sell at distressed prices to get out of what looks like a declining situation. After a period of time, things change. Earnings begin to increase or accelerate. The public notices the improvement, and buyers of the stock bid the price back up to or above intrinsic worth. The value investor buys the stock when it is low, hopefully, and sells when it is at or above intrinsic value.

Some of these value investors call themselves *contrarians*. They act contrary to the prevailing public sentiment. If the public sentiment on a stock is negative because of unfavorable reports such as poor earnings, then the nervous shareholders sell their shares at lower and lower prices. The contrarians buy the stock at low, bargain level prices despite the bad publicity and negative sentiment.

Growth style

Growth managers have an entirely different style. Growth investors look for stocks with rapidly increasing earnings per share or stocks which are expected to show rapidly increasing earnings per share in the foreseeable future. If such growth can be sustained over a period of years, the price of the stock will reward its investors by increasing. Usually, the most successful growth investors buy the stock early on, when the stock is just a few years old. Of course, the risk at this stage is quite high. Other growth investors can be successful in buying well-established stocks as long as the growth continues into the future, and the investors don't over pay for the stock.

Growth stocks generally have high price-earnings ratios, high price to book value ratios, high price volatility, and low dividend payout ratios.

Momentum investing is a variation of the growth style. It's the growth style with more than average risk. Momentum investors buy stocks which have increasing earnings along with an increasing price per share. As long as the news about a stock continues to get better and better and as long as the stock keeps going up, they buy the stock. They bet on winners, so to speak. In the extreme, the price they have to pay for the stock is not a factor. As long as the news is good, they keep buying the stock as it goes up. As soon as earnings come in below estimates or stock analysts reduce their estimates of future earnings, the momentum investors or fund managers sell the stock. The problem is that everybody wants to sell at the same time. The risk is that the stock may go down 20 to 30 percent or more in a single day before the investor is able to sell.

The value style, the growth style, and the momentum variation of the growth style can perform well. Usually, one style significantly outperforms the other style for a few years and then the situation reverses. Most fund managers use one of these styles almost exclusively.

The blended style is a cross between growth and value. Managers of funds with a blended style seek fast growth, but they want to buy it at a bargain price. A few managers provide a blended portfolio with some growth stocks and some value stocks.

Size categories
Another distinction among stock mutual funds is the size of the companies in the investment portfolio. Corporate size is measured by

market capitalization, which is the number of shares outstanding times the current price per share. In other words, market capitalization is the total market value of all the shares of a company's stock. There are three size categories: small, mid, and large. There are no standard definitions of these terms. Roughly, the sizes are as follows:

small-cap stocks – companies with capitalization of less than $1 billion
mid-cap stocks – companies with capitalization of $1 bil. to $5 bil.
large-cap stocks – companies with capitalization of more than $5 bil.

Historically, small-cap stocks have outperformed the other two categories. The larger gains of small-cap stocks were accompanied by larger risks. But, as with any historical reference to investment performance, history is not doomed to repeat itself. During some periods, small-cap stocks have done rather poorly in comparison to large-cap stocks. Such is the case as the 1990s draw to a close. But that's not surprising. Trends change back and forth.

Although many stock funds have the very same objective, those funds may use different investment styles and buy stock in different size companies. Consequently, there are many different categories of stock funds. The differences among the various categories are quite substantial. While one or two types may be quite suitable for you, some of the other categories may be entirely unsuitable. The rest of this section on stock funds covers the various subcategories within the stock fund category.

Investment objective categories
Aggressive growth funds seek maximum capital gains as their single objective. Current dividend income is not a factor. Most of these funds use the growth or momentum style. Some of these funds use specialized securities and trading techniques such as: options, futures, short sales, etc. An explanation of these specialized techniques is beyond the scope of this book. Suffice it to say that these techniques usually attempt to increase performance, while adding more risk. Sometimes these funds are labeled as capital appreciation funds.

Growth funds also seek capital gains as their single objective. Managers of growth funds seek less risk in their investments than do the managers of aggressive growth funds. Most growth funds use the growth style of investing, and most of them invest in large-cap or mid-cap stocks.

Growth and Income funds seek a combination of both growth and dividend income. Many of these fund managers use the value style of investing, while some use the growth style or a balance of the two styles. Most of the portfolio investments are large-cap or mid-cap stocks. Be aware that some funds may describe themselves to be in one category but may act like another category. A minority of funds in the growth and income category actually act more like growth funds than growth and income funds.

Income-equity funds seek a high level of current income by investing primarily in stocks with high dividend payout ratios. Over time, these stocks may also increase in value as dividends on these stocks increase. Typically, the dividend portion of the total return is greater than the growth (capital appreciation) portion. The reverse is true for growth and income funds. Income-equity funds tend to fluctuate inversely with interest rates. In that regard they act like long-term bond funds which go up in value when interest rates decline. They tend to drop in price when interest rates increase.

Index funds. Portfolio managers of index funds design their portfolios to match as closely as possible the results of a stock market index. These funds do not attempt to "beat the market." They attempt to approximate the market indexes by owning the same stocks that are in the indexes. Since these funds do not need a team of investment analysts, these funds have lower expense ratios than the standard actively managed funds. The gross investment performance before expenses should be about the same for the index and the index mutual funds. The low fund expenses then result in the mutual fund's performance being only slightly below the index. We'll have more to say about index funds in Chapter 11.

Small company growth funds. These funds invest in small-cap companies. Quite often, these companies have developed new and innovative products for the marketplace. The shares of these small companies may be thinly traded. Good news can quickly increase the prices for these stocks, but bad news can devastate the stocks in a single day. As with all other investment categories, this category is sometimes in favor for a few years and then out of favor. When it's out of favor, these stocks can go down even as other categories are going up. Nevertheless, over the long-term, this category has significantly outperformed the other categories.

International funds seek capital gains by investing in common stocks of companies located outside the United States. These funds must invest at least 65% of their portfolios in international stocks at all times to be classified as international funds. Since some foreign economies often grow faster than the U. S. economy, international funds have the potential to outperform conventional domestic funds. Of course, the risk can be greater, as well. Normal business risks on stocks outside the U.S. are greater than for U.S. stocks because many foreign countries do not require their corporations to provide investors with full disclosure of information. In addition to the normal business risks and market risks, there are currency exchange rate risks and political risks due to unstable governments. Some of these funds specialize in a region, such as Asia. Others specialize in single countries. The more specialized the fund, the less diversification and greater risk it has.

Combination funds. By policy, combination funds can own a mix of U.S. and international common stocks, bonds, and/or other assets.

Global equity funds seek growth or capital appreciation by investing in both international stocks and domestic common stocks. Mutual funds in this category use both the value and growth styles of investing. They also buy all sizes of stocks: small-cap, mid-cap, and large-cap. Usually the greatest percentage of investments is in U.S. stocks. The percentage in U.S. stocks may be more or less than 50%. Fund managers seek out the best investments they can find worldwide.

Balanced funds are similar to growth and income funds in that these funds seek both growth and income. The difference is that balanced funds have a mix of common stocks, preferred stocks, and bonds in the portfolio. Growth and income funds may use only stocks in the portfolio. For investors who don't like the risk of putting all their money into stocks or all into bonds, a balanced fund is a good way to diversify.

Asset allocation funds may be 100% invested in stocks or bonds or money market investments. Or they may be invested in two or all three of the above types of investments depending on what the portfolio manager believes will produce optimum results. These funds are also called flexible portfolio funds because the portfolio manager can be totally flexible in how he or she allocates the fund's assets. Depending on fund policy, these funds may invest in international stocks, gold stocks, convertible bonds, or any other securities as stated in the fund's prospectus.

Income-Mixed funds seek a high level of current income by investing in both bonds and income producing stocks.

Convertible securities funds. These funds invest in bonds or preferred stocks which can be converted into the common stock of the issuing corporation. For example, a $1000 convertible bond could be converted into 50 shares of stock. If the market price of the stock goes up sharply, the price of the bond will follow along with it. A disadvantage of convertible securities is that they pay out lower current dividends or interest income than non-convertible securities of the same issuing corporation. There's always a tradeoff. Also, these securities often have higher than average credit risk. Some issuers allow their preferred stocks or bonds to have the convertible feature because the issuing companies are risky. Without the "sweetener" of the convertible feature, the issuing companies wouldn't be able to sell the securities.

Specialty funds. Specialty funds have a very narrow field of securities to invest in. Therefore, by definition, they are not well diversified. They entail greater risk and the possibility of a greater return than standard diversified funds. Specialty funds can often be found on lists of the top performing funds, as well as on lists of worst performing funds.

Although specialty funds are high risk funds, it doesn't follow that conservative investors should necessarily avoid them completely. A conservative investor may own several mutual funds. While such an investor may put 85% or 90% of his or her money into well diversified mutual funds, the investor may want to put 10% or 15% of assets into specialty funds. The specialty funds can add greater diversification to the total portfolio of funds the investor owns. These funds may also enhance the total return on the overall portfolio. Some investors may have expert knowledge of the industry they work in. They can spot business trends in their industry even before professional investment analysts can. When economic conditions in such an industry start changing for the better, the investor could feel comfortable in buying that specialty mutual fund. Novice investors should be very careful about buying specialty funds. Often novice investors are attracted to a specialty fund after it appears at the top of a list of best performing funds. Beware. The greatest growth for that fund is probably nothing but history at that point. After one or two years at the top of the list, that specialty fund is almost certain to under perform the rest of the stock market.

The following categories include most types of specialty funds.

Industry funds. Numerous industries have mutual funds which specialize in that one industry. These are sometimes called *sector funds*. Some of the more popular industry funds are: energy stock funds, environmental securities funds, health and biotechnology securities funds, real estate securities funds, technology securities funds, utilities funds. Gold and precious metals funds are also industry funds; however, since they have been around for so much longer than the other industry funds, they are usually separately classified.

Gold and precious metals funds. These funds seek to achieve capital appreciation by investing at least 65% of their assets in securities associated with gold, silver, and other precious metals. The securities are typically common stocks of gold or silver mining companies.

Gold and silver mining companies almost always have high production costs. For example, at some gold mines it may cost $330 an ounce to mine the gold. If the market price of gold increases from $340 an ounce to $360 an ounce, the profits triple from $10 an ounce to $30 an ounce. If this happens, the per share earnings of the stocks dramatically increase. The per share stock prices also tend to go up when the earnings increase. This leverage works on both the upside and downside making these stocks highly volatile. In some one-year periods or even three or five year periods, gold funds have dominated the list of best performing mutual funds in all categories. In other periods, they have been at the very bottom of performance rankings. Historically, over most periods of 10 years and longer, these funds have not performed as well as the other categories.

Special objective funds. With these funds, it's not so much what they invest in but what they refuse to invest in. They generally avoid alcohol and tobacco companies. Additionally, they may avoid companies with pollution problems, large military contracts, etc. The idea is to ensure investors that the companies represented in a fund's portfolio do not violate the investors' values.

U.S. regional securities funds. These funds concentrate on securities of companies headquartered in a specific region of the country. The idea is that local investment analysts and portfolio managers can be the most knowledgeable about these companies, particularly the smaller companies in the area.

Other classification systems

There is no universally accepted system of mutual fund classification. Different financial publications use a few different categories than the ones described above. For stock funds, most of the other categories relate to capitalization (small, mid, or large) and style of investing (growth, value, or blend). For bond funds, most of the other categories relate to average length of maturity of bonds in the portfolio (long-term, intermediate-term, or short-term). Understanding these classification systems in terms of risk is fairly straightforward. Generally, larger cap stocks are less risky than small caps, and value style is less risky than growth style. Short-term bonds are less risky than long-term bonds.

Conclusion

Stocks and bonds are complicated; but mutual funds, even though they sound complex, will provide the simplicity you desire. You may be feeling overwhelmed at this point. That's OK. Simplicity does await you near the end of Chapter 11! But next, we cover the difficult and complex topic of risk.

CHAPTER 9

RISK AND RETURN

Risk is Slippery.

As we've already stated, risk is directly related to return. No one will voluntarily assume extra risk without the possibility of achieving greater return. So, the rate of return must be compared to the degree of risk in order to evaluate the effectiveness of any investment. Fortunately, the rate of return can be quantified, but risk is a far more elusive concept. This chapter concentrates on the shifting and slippery concept of risk.

Risk means different things to different people. Objectively speaking, a young person can assume more risk than an older person because if the young person suffers a loss, that person has many more years of active living to make up the loss. But, some young people simply cannot emotionally tolerate much risk. On the other hand, some older people enjoy and thrive on high risks. In order to measure risk tolerance, some organizations have developed questionnaires. Yet, none of these questionnaires or any other techniques are totally reliable and accurate. Additionally, a person's risk tolerance may change as time passes, as his or her knowledge grows, as income levels go up or down, and as the news and other people influence the investor. For instance, in a down market, the investor is likely to be overly concerned with risk, as negative stories come out in the news. As friends and relatives complain about losing money with their investments, a person's willingness to assume risks tends to change. Looking at it from the standpoint of the investor, risk is quite slippery, so to speak.

Looking at risk from the standpoint of the investment is less slippery, but it still amounts to making estimates of the unknown. You may have come across these terms: beta, standard deviation, alpha, Sharpe Index, etc. These terms of statistical analysis help investors compare the risks of various investments. However, it is important to realize that these statistics measure past performance and past risks. The past is no guarantee of the future in our ever changing world. We can estimate the future by analyzing the past, but we cannot be entirely accurate in doing so. No one has yet invented a totally reliable set of mathematical formulas that can predict future risk or future performance.

The investor has several inexact tasks to perform with regard to risk management. First, the investor must measure his or her risk tolerance level. Second, the investor must analyze the various degrees of risks in alternative investments. Third, the investor needs to match his or her risk tolerance level to the investments which have that level of risk. Hopefully, those investments will provide enough return to meet the investor's goals. If not, the investor may need to stretch out of his or her comfort zone to assume a little more risk. If that doesn't work, the investor may need to lower his or her goals.

There is another alternative. An investor can possibly increase the rate of return without increasing risk. This could be done by optimum investment selection. We'll consider that option later. But, first, what is risk?

What is Risk?

The possibility of loss

From the investor's standpoint, risk can be any number of things. Risk can mean the probability or odds of losing money. The greater the potential loss in dollars, the greater the risk. Also, the greater the probability of any loss, the greater the risk. Any loss at all, even a small loss, is a blow to the investor's ego. For example, Martha would feel bad about a $1000 investment declining to $980 at the end of a year. Martha would say to herself: "I was so stupid to take my money out of the bank. I could have earned a guaranteed 5.00% or $50 if only I had left the money in CDs. Why did I believe George when he said I should take the risk? Look where it got me!" Psychologically, Martha is beating herself up and feels inadequate about herself for having made what she now believes was a dumb decision.

Feelings play a major role in the investor's perception of risk. Studies show that investors feel joy when they make profitable investments. But when investors make unprofitable investments, they feel psychological pain. What's more, the pain of a loss is much stronger than the joy of a gain for most investors. No wonder, then, that many investors are quite fearful of the stock market. For many or most investors, if a stock or mutual fund declines below the investor's purchase price, the investor will not sell at a loss. Instead, the investor will hold on to that investment for however many years it takes for the investment to go back up to the investor's cost. At that time, the investor will sell the investment and "get out whole." The pain of taking a loss is so great that the investor will hold on for years just to break even on the investment. Of course, merely breaking even is a very poor investment return. No matter. The investor avoids the psychological pain of taking a loss. Where risk is concerned, feelings are usually stronger than logic. Logic would dictate holding the stock for another six months or a year, at least. The stock has been down a long time and is now finally improving; momentum is certainly favorable. Since there was a good reason to buy the stock in the first place, that reason is even more compelling now. Logically, it is probably a very good buy or hold at this point. But most investors are glad to be out of this stock finally. They are relieved to get this experience behind them. Thankfully, they avoided the emotional pain of having to sell at a loss. It's human nature to avoid pain. If the investor had held the stock after it reached the break-even point and the stock subsequently declined again, the pain would be all the greater. Can't you hear Martha beating up on herself? "I can't believe I was this stupid. I had my chance to get out of that dog with no loss. But what did I do? I held onto it like an idiot!" Most investors are not going to take the chance that the stock might drop a second time. Being wrong once is bad enough. Twice, no way. Logic is not a factor; it's all emotion.

The uncertainty of gain

While the possibility of loss is the predominate view of risk, there are other views. The uncertainty of future gains is another. Will the investment produce the desired total ending amount? It's a risk. The goal might or might not be reached. How important is the goal to you? If the goal is a trip around the world every four years, missing that goal is not a huge risk. With somewhat less than expected investment performance, the investor might have to cut back to one trip every eight years. If the goal is to have enough money at age 85, the uncertainty of not reaching that goal can have high emotional and physical consequences. If investment performance is somewhat less than expected, the investor could totally run out of money long before age 85. At age 75, this retiree might have to substantially curtail his or her lifestyle and perhaps be forced to take an unpleasant job to make ends meet. Risk can mean the possibility of loss on the one hand and the uncertainty of gain on the other hand. At first glance, these views seem to be totally different. In reality, both risks actually amount to being out of money. Many people pay too much attention to the risk of loss now and not enough attention to the possible lack of money later.

What if you buy the investment after it has already gone up as high as its going to go? There's a risk that bad timing could cost you plenty. If you think market prices are high right now, you might sell and wait for a decline before reinvesting. But what if the market goes up after you sell. There's a risk of being out of the market. In the stock market, the entire gain for a three-year period could be realized in three weeks. If you missed out on that big three-week rally, you might not reach your long term goals.

Volatility of prices

Volatility of prices is another view of risk. Something that's up 40% one year, down 35% the next year, and so on is risky. What if I need the money when it's down sharply? I might have to sell a good investment at a loss.

We've stated three views of risk from the investor's standpoint: the possibility of loss, uncertainty of gain, volatility of prices. All three are valid views of risk. All of these views involve the investor's feelings.

It's so easy to advise you to forget your feelings and operate on logic only. But, of course, that won't work. Inevitably, feelings will play a major part in how much risk you will take. It is important, though, that you also bring knowledgeable, informed logic into your investment decisions as best you can. Obviously, the intent of much of this book is to help you do just that.

Types of Risk

The major categories of risks are *systematic risks* and *unsystematic risks*. Systematic risks affect markets across the board. Unsystematic risks affect only individual stocks and bonds.

Systematic risks

The systematic risks are: purchasing power risk, interest rate risk, market risk, and political risk. We've already covered purchasing power risk (inflation risk) and interest rate risk. To recap briefly, purchasing power risk is the possibility that the prices of consumer goods and services will increase faster than the gains on your investments. Interest rate risk is the decrease in bond prices when interest rates rise. There's no way to eliminate all risk. You can only manage risk.

Market risk is the possibility that even good investments will decline when the overall market declines. The saying, "a rising tide lifts all boats" works both ways. Market risk is caused by investor reaction to general news items. Most stocks are affected to some degree even though the news may not relate to a particular stock.

Political risk is the possibility of unfavorable government actions in a country. Unfavorable actions include the following: seizure of assets, exchange control laws, war, anarchy, etc. Political risks are greatest in developing countries. The United States is considered to be the country with the least political risk. Like market risk, political risk affects all investments in the country. These risks affect the entire system or all securities; hence they are called systematic risks.

Unsystematic risks

Other risks relate to investments in a single company's securities. These are called unsystematic risks. The most important of these are business risk, financial risk, credit risk, and liquidity risk. Since this book recommends investments in mutual funds rather than individual securities, it is sufficed to say that business risk, financial risk, default risk and credit risk relate to the strength and stability of an individual company. These risks are low for large, profitable, low debt companies in stable industries.

Liquidity risk is low if an asset can be sold quickly at its current market value. If a sale takes a long time or has to be made at a substantially reduced price, liquidity risk is high. Mutual funds can invest a small portion of their assets in securities with high liquidity risk. However, mutual fund shares have a low liquidity risk. Generally, funds send out redemption checks within seven days after request is received. The Redemption of Shares section in the fund's prospectus has complete details.

Measuring Investment Risk

The various types of risk described above create the possibility of loss as well as the potential for gain. How much loss, how much gain, and what are the probabilities or odds? Risk is not simply the potential for losing principal. Risk is the variation or volatility of returns both up and down. Technical, statistical analysis is used to evaluate risks. In this section, we'll simplify and summarize the research as it relates to mutual fund investments. With a general understanding of a few terms described below, you'll be a much more knowledgeable investor.

Mean return

Perhaps the easiest risk/reward term to understand is *mean return*. The mean return is the average return. So, if a stock or a mutual fund is up 12% in year one, down 5% in year two and up 8% in year three, the average or mean return is (+12-5+8) divided by three years equals 5%. Another investment has returns of +6%, +5%, and +4% over three years. The average for the second investment, Fund B, is also 5%.

Standard deviation

Intuitively, we know that Fund A above was riskier than Fund B. Fund A fluctuated more; it had returns further away from the mean than did Fund B. Statisticians quantify these variations or fluctuations. The basic term used to describe the variations is "standard deviation." I don't want to elaborate on mathematics and statistics so much that you become bored or frustrated; so I'm leaving out the formula and calculations of standard deviation. Suffice it to say that the greater the standard deviation, the greater the volatility or risk. The smaller the standard deviation, the closer the actual results are to the average.

Correlation

The next important term is *correlation*. Correlation measures how closely two investments perform in relation to each other. If both investments move in tandem with each other, the correlation is +1. Moving in tandem means when Investment A is up 10%, Investment B is also up 10%; when A is down 6%, B is also down 6% etc. Correlation figures range from +1, which is perfect association, to 0, meaning they have no relationship to each other, to -1, meaning they have an inverse or opposite relationship. A correlation of -1 means that when A is up 8%, B is down 8%, etc. In the real world, there are no -1 correlations. Most investment correlations are between 0 and +1.

Combining two investments with low correlations reduces the volatility of the combined portfolio. When the correlation is low, both investments are unlikely to go down in tandem with each other. The better performance of one investment partially offsets the worse performance of the other. The result is lower volatility of the overall portfolio, which means lower risk for the portfolio. A diversified portfolio of 20 or more securities with low correlation virtually eliminates the risk of disaster happening to the portfolio as a result of the performance of one security in the portfolio.

Because diversification substantially reduces the risks associated with a single security, the importance and benefits of diversification cannot be overstated.

Beta

Once the unsystematic risks are controlled by diversification that leaves the systematic risks to deal with. These risks can drive down the value of an entire portfolio. Perhaps the most important systematic risk for investors in U.S. common stocks is market risk. Market risk is good news or bad news that tends to move all stocks up or down. Negative or "bearish" market risk does put downward pressure even on strong stocks, and positive or "bullish" market risk puts upward pressure even on weak stocks. Of course, not every single stock will move in the same direction.

Beta is the term statisticians use to measure systematic risk. Beta uses standard deviation in its formula. Once again, it's the concept rather than the mathematics that is important here. In the context of mutual fund investments, beta indicates how much a fund is likely to go up or down in response to the movement of the overall market. So, Martha might ask, "If the market goes down 10%, how much is my fund likely to go down?" Beta answers that question. Beta is the change in the return of a specific fund divided by the change in the return on the market. Therefore, if the market goes down 10%, a fund with a beta of 1.00 should also go down 10%. If the beta is .9, the fund should go down 9% in response to a 10% drop in the market. If the market is up 10%, a fund with a beta of 2.0 should go up 20%. In other words, multiply beta times the return on the market to get expected return of the fund. Beta is relevant when the overall portfolio or fund has a high correlation to the market. High correlation to the market is achieved with broad diversi- fication. A fund of gold mining stocks would not have broad diversification. Beta would be worthless in evaluating risk of a gold fund.

If you want to avoid a high risk fund, do not invest in a fund which has a very high beta. Once again, don't forget the old caution that statistics measure the past. Betas can and do change in the future. Nevertheless, for a well diversified mutual fund with continuity of management, the beta is fairly stable.

Risk-Adjusted Returns and Ratings

Now let's summarize; risk is volatility as measured by standard deviation and beta. Investors take on more risk in order to achieve greater returns. But Martha is tired of all this theory. She asks, "Why should I pay good money to bright mutual fund managers if the returns are based solely on mathematics rather than skill. Aren't some portfolio managers better than other managers? Aren't the best fund managers better at picking good stocks than average managers?" She says, "What I want is a fund that performs much better than other funds with the same degree of risk." Martha does not merely want a good return on her investment; she wants a good risk-adjusted return. Another way of looking at risk-adjusted returns is to desire a fund which has much less volatility (risk) than other funds which earn the same return. Wouldn't you rather have Fund B in the earlier example, which earned 6% in year one, 5% in year two, and 4% in year three than Fund A, which also averaged 5% but had one loss year in its results? On a risk-adjusted basis, Fund B is superior to Fund A. Intuitively, we know this. But can it be quantified? Yes. The Sharpe Ratio or Sharpe Index quantifies risk-adjusted performance. Additionally, alpha, otherwise known as Jensen's Alpha or Jensen's Index, also quantifies risk-adjusted performance.

The Sharpe Ratio relates the return on a fund to the total degree of risk in the fund. The higher the ratio or index, the greater the return for each unit of risk. By definition, a mutual fund with a higher Sharpe Ratio than the Sharpe Ratio of the entire market beats the market on a risk/return basis.

Alpha, or Jensen's Alpha, is an easier risk-adjusted concept to deal with, in my opinion. Here's the concept. Statisticians determine how much return a fund should earn for a given level of volatility (risk). They compare that expected return with the actual return. The difference is called alpha. In other words, did the fund do better or worse than average in comparison with funds of similar volatility (risk)? If the average return of those equal risk funds was 9% and Fund A earned 8%, then Fund A has an alpha of -1.00%. The manager's security selection was less than average. Likewise, if Fund A earned 15.5%, the alpha is +6.5%. Any positive alpha means the fund outperformed the market on a risk-adjusted basis. The higher the alpha, the better.

Morningstar, which is a leading mutual fund evaluation and rating service, publishes the above risk statistics for each of the funds it evaluates. Morningstar also provides risk-adjusted performance ratings in the form of stars. A five star rating is its highest risk-adjusted rating.

How to Reduce Risk

Diversify. That point cannot be overstated. Even the brightest and most well-informed investors are wrong some of the time. That's why prudence dictates that even the top professionals don't put all their money into their best investment idea. Those one or two best ideas could turn out very badly. If so, the investor loses most of his or her capital. The investor no longer has the capital to put into other good investments. He or she has to start all over. For an older investor, the result is disastrous. Gone is most or all of the savings of a lifetime. Gone is the opportunity to enjoy the luxuries of life. Gone is the opportunity to offer financial help to family members or favorite charities. In times of prosperity, it is all too easy to believe that these things can't happen.

The risk/return ratio is poor for undiversified investors. There is a small chance of greater returns but a much larger increase in risk. So, is it necessary to own two or more mutual funds to be properly diversified? No, not at all. A single, well-diversified fund can be quite sufficient.

Dollar cost averaging is an additional technique to reduce your risk and increase your return. Dollar cost averaging is simply investing equal sums of money at regular intervals. The intervals should be relatively short, at least as often as quarterly, or even better monthly. The best dollar cost averaging strategy is to invest a little from your paycheck each pay period. This strategy allows you to average into a market and in most cases to achieve a lower average cost per share. When prices are low, your money will buy more shares. When prices are high, your money will purchase fewer shares of the investment. The result is that there are more shares of low-priced stock and fewer shares of high-priced stock in your portfolio. That reduces the average price per share in your portfolio. Since dollar cost averaging works best for investments which have large price variations, the volatility can actually work in your favor. The method works even better when there is some long term upward movement in the price of the investment.

Dollar cost averaging mitigates or reduces the distress of seeing your investment fall in price. The emotional impact of market downturns is reduced. The lower price is now seen as a good opportunity to acquire more shares at low cost.

In the real world, as your paycheck increases over time, your periodic investment will also increase; therefore, you won't be investing exactly equal amounts over your entire working period. Although dollar cost averaging calls for equal investments, you'll get roughly the same results with gradually increasing periodic investments.

Appendix E shows an example of dollar cost averaging. For those of you who don't like tables of numbers, I'll summarize the results here so you won't need to study the table. In that example, the beginning and ending price per share in the market was 16, and the average price per share during the period was $16.16. Nevertheless, due to dollar cost averaging, the average cost of shares was only $15.84.

Timing the market is an alternative to dollar cost averaging. You could save your money in the bank until you believed the market was about to go up sharply. At that point, you could take all your money out of the bank and invest it at what you believe is a good (low) price. You could try to "time the market" by investing all your money when prices were low and then selling out when prices were high. After the sale, you would then put your money back in the bank, waiting for the next opportunity to buy low again. By correctly "timing the market" over the course of several market cycles, you could get much better performance than by holding onto your dollar cost averaged shares. Although timing the market sounds like a great idea from a theoretical standpoint, it is risky and not a good idea for several reasons.

The main reason it is not a good idea is that nobody has a perfect crystal ball. Many investors have tried to time the market with the help of market newsletters or market timing services. During some market periods, some investors have been able to increase their returns. However, based on the reports I've seen, market timing for the most part does not produce successful results. It does produce a lot of risk. One risk is being out of the market too long waiting for the market to go down. You can miss out on substantial gains quickly when you're out of the market. Often, most of the gains of an entire year occur over a short few weeks.

Another problem is that it is very hard emotionally to commit all of your funds at one time. You might be investing at the wrong time. If you try to time the market, your emotions will work against you.

It's all too easy to invest when everybody has been doing so well for a number of years. When all the financial news is good, it seems you can't lose. Yet, that's the time when prices are already high. Usually, the best time to buy is when the financial news is bad. When things are bad, the market psychology is that things may get a whole lot worse. At that time prices are low, but nobody feels good about buying.

If you really have to try timing the market, set aside a small portion of your money for this strategy. Use dollar cost averaging with the greatest part of your assets.

With dollar cost averaging, you are forced to buy more shares at low prices and fewer shares at high prices. You put your plan into effect, and you do it NOW. If you don't start putting a little money in the market now, there's a good chance you won't take the risk with more money later. For most people, the very best way to reduce risk is to **Pay yourself first and do it now.**

Prudent holding periods can reduce risk. The longer you can commit to investing in stock or bond funds, the lower the risk of loss of principal. Consider the historical record illustrated below.

Table 9-1
Number of periods with negative performance, 1926 to 1997.
Worst Performance by Holding Periods, 1926 to 1997.
The period of that worst performance.

Performance is compounded annual rates of return in percent.

Periods	20 yr	10 yr	5 yr	1 yr
Large Company				
# of periods negative	0 of 53	2 of 63	7 of 68	20 of 72
Worst performance	+3.11%	-0.89%	-12.47%	-43.34%
Worst period	1929-48	1929-38	1928-32	1931
Small Company				
# of periods negative	0 of 53	2 of 63	9 of 68	21 of 72
Worst performance	+5.74%	-5.70%	-27.54%	-58.01%
Worst period	1929-48	1929-38	1928-32	1937
Intermediate-term government bonds				
# of periods negative	0 of 53	0 of 63	0 of 68	7 of 72
Worst performance	+1.58%	+1.25%	+0.96%	-5.14%
Worst period	1940-59	1947-56	1955-59	1944

As you can see from Table 9-1, investment performance in a single year can be nearly disastrous. However, if you can hold the investment for ten years, the results demonstrate that risk is substantially reduced. After twenty years, all results have been positive. Thus, young investors can view stock and bond investments as not very risky if they can and will stay in the market in bad times as well as good times.

The greater the number of years in the holding period of an investment, the higher the odds of actually getting theoretical results. The theoretical result is that stock and bond investments make a profit. (Of course, this statement assumes a properly diversified portfolio.)

Additionally, the longer the holding period, the closer the actual results should approximate historical results. In a single year, the stock market could drop 20% or more. In a five-year period, the market could drop 10% or more. Yet, the longer the period, the closer the actual results will come to the theoretical results. After twenty years, the market should increase roughly the same percentage as it did in a previous twenty-year period.

The longer the time period, the less relevant beta is. If you're going to hold an investment for 20 or 30 years, what difference does it make how much it fluctuates up and down during the holding period? After 20 or 30 years, the ending result should be close to the theoretical result anyway. So it had more ups and downs getting there. So what. The ending result is what really matters. If you're not going to cash out until the end of the 20 or 30-year period, volatility and beta lose their importance from a logical standpoint.

Risk Tolerance Level

Hopefully, the above logic will somewhat influence your emotions. However, don't expect logic to radically change your emotions. Hear what Martha has to say to George. "I know the market is not supposed to go down for the next thirty years. But, George, we could be going into a real depression. The market is down 20% from when we started investing. Some companies in town are laying off employees. The financial writers predict more losses in the stock market. How do we know we're in the right mutual fund? Maybe we should be in the most conservative fund we can find. I think we should just get out now and put our money in the bank where it will be safe. George, I'm scared. We can't afford to take these losses."

Like it or not, emotions do play a big role in investing. Besides, Martha has a point. How can she be sure that their mutual fund is a good one? Should they stick with the fund they have or exchange it into another, hopefully better, fund? Or should they just sell out?

George and Martha are young enough to invest with a 30-year time horizon. Yet that doesn't mean they should own highly volatile investments. George and Martha must be emotionally comfortable with their investments in down periods as well as up periods. Obviously, they will be more comfortable in up periods. If they would be quite upset about a 20% market decline, they should not be in investments which historically experience occasional 20% declines. If they do get into such a situation, they will either sell at a 20% loss or wait until the investment goes back up to their cost and then sell. In either case, their holding period is substantially reduced. George and Martha should evaluate their risk tolerance level, and they should take on as much risk as they can comfortably tolerate but not more than they can deal with. As they get much older, their time horizon will shorten and thus their risk level should also decline.

What is your risk tolerance level? How much risk are you comfortable with? How much risk is too much for you to emotionally handle? How much risk is it prudent for you to take on? Easy questions to ask. Hard questions to answer.

The following attitudes and behaviors indicate a relatively high risk profile:

1. Willingness to go into debt
2. Owning your own business or making frequent job changes
3. Having confidence in your decisions

4. Being more concerned with potential gains than potential losses
5. Feeling optimistic about life

Rank the following in order of importance to you, one being the most important and four the least important.

1. Avoidance of capital loss
2. Low volatility of market value
3. Capital appreciation
4. Inflation protection

If avoidance of capital loss is number one and low volatility of market value is number two, then you probably should put your investments into CDs and high-grade short or intermediate-term bond funds. If inflation protection and capital appreciation are ranked one and two, then you should invest in the stock market.

Answer the following three questions True or False.

I want to be in the stock market when it goes up. However, it is more important to me to be out of the stock market when it goes down.

I definitely need to avoid stock market declines. I plan to avoid losses by "timing the market." When the stock market is about to drop, I'll sell stocks and buy CDs. When the stock market is ready to go up, I'll sell CDs and buy stocks.

If the stock market declines and stays down for four years, I'll surely know that my stock market investments were a bad idea, and I would sell immediately or as soon as my investments reach break even point.

Answering true to any of the three questions indicates a relatively low risk profile. Certainly, most people want to avoid unnecessary risks. With investments, there is no way to avoid risk. If you avoid the risk of stock market investments, you may risk losing your desired lifestyle after retirement. Low risk investments may not produce enough resources to achieve the lifestyle you want. You may even run out of savings and investments after retirement, if your investments don't grow enough now.

CHAPTER 10

ASSET ALLOCATION in IRA and 401(k)

The purpose of this chapter is to provide guidance in how to allocate contributions into your IRA or 401(k) plan. Therefore, it is useful to understand why an investment should be matched both to the investor's risk profile and to the investor's goal. The goal of your IRA or 401(k) is to provide substantial funds to meet your needs and goals after retirement. For young people this goal is long-term. For short-term goals, like your next vacation, stock market investments are not appropriate. They are too risky. Therefore, it is important to have different types of investments earmarked for different goals. The most conservative investors will want money market funds or bank CDs for both short-term goals and long-term goals. Those investors who are willing to assume more risk will utilize mostly stocks for their IRAs, while using CDs for short-term goals.

Matching Risks

Asset allocation is the process of matching your risk level to the level of risk in your investments. The lower your risk tolerance, the greater the percentage of your investments should be in asset classes with historically low downside risk or volatility. Additionally, if your risk tolerance is low, you should ideally be invested in more than one asset class. Three major asset classes are: domestic stocks, bonds, and cash equivalents (Treasury bills, certificates of deposit, or money market funds). Some other important asset classes are international stocks, precious metals, and real estate. The greater your risk tolerance level, the greater the percentage of your assets should be in asset classes with

150

historically high returns. Diversification across asset classes is not a requirement for those with high risk tolerance.

Historic Asset Class Returns

Stocks have performed better than bonds, and bonds have performed better than Treasury bills (T-bills) over long term periods. Also, over long term periods, the risks have been highest for stocks, less for bonds, and least for T-bills. Virtually all experts are highly confident that stocks will continue to outperform bonds and bonds will continue to do better than T-bills and other cash equivalents over the long term. Considering these broad categories, history has proven to be a very reliable guide to the future.

The major asset categories which are appropriate for IRAs and 401(k) plans are U.S. stocks, bonds, and money market assets. Additionally, global stocks and bonds can be appropriate but should not constitute the majority of assets in retirement plans. Other asset classes, such as real estate and commodities, can be appropriate for some investors outside of retirement accounts; however these asset classes don't belong in 401(k) accounts and IRAs.

The following table shows the annual compound rates of return and standard deviations for the major asset classes and compares those rates to the rate of inflation.

Table 10-1
Investment Performance 1926 to 1997

	Compounded Annual Return	Standard Deviation
Large company stocks	11.0%	20.3%
Small company stocks	12.7	33.9
Long-term corporate bonds	5.7	8.7
Long-term government bonds	5.2	9.2
Intermediate-term government bonds	5.3	5.7
U.S. Treasury Bills	3.8	3.2
Inflation	3.1	4.5

Used with permission. © 1998 Ibbotson Associates, Inc. All rights reserved. [Certain portions of this work were derived from copyrighted works of Roger Ibbotson and Rex Sinquefield.]

As you can see from Table 10-1, small cap stocks have performed better than large cap stocks in the 1926 to 1997 period. However, the risk in small cap stocks is far greater than the risk in large cap stocks. What Table 10-1 doesn't show is that in some periods between 1926 and 1997, large caps performed better than small caps.

In recent years, investment gains have been far above the historical averages. In the five-year period 1993 to 1997, large cap stocks have enjoyed 20.24% compounded annual gains, while small caps have returned 19.35% annually.

Historically, during prolonged periods of stock market prosperity, investors have believed that the good times would last forever, or at least quite a few more years – with no end in sight. Inevitably, the good times come to an end. Are things any different now? Will the stock market not have a 20% or 30% or even 40% decline sometime in the lifetime of today's young people? If history is a guide, young people can expect to see some steep declines. They can also expect that the above-average performance of the stock market for the five and ten years ending in 1997 will settle somewhere near long-term historical averages.

Investment Size and Style

In a sense, the stock market is like the fashion industry. Fads come and go; styles come and go. In the stock market, it's called *leadership* or *rotation*. Economic news causes a group of stocks to be very popular for a time. Those leading stocks become relatively overvalued due to the market psychology. Other stocks in comparison are undervalued. After a time, a different group takes the lead with rapidly increasing stock prices. The change in leadership occurs over and over. In other words, in any stock market environment, some groups of stocks do better than others. After a time, the groups that previously lagged behind start doing better than the previous favorites.

Many trends occur in the stock market. One trend is based on the size, or total market value, of a stock. The large-cap stock category may be the favorite for a period. During other years, mid-cap or small-cap stocks perform best. The same phenomenon occurs in down markets, as well. One group may go down much more than the other groups. One way to reduce risk is to have a fund which has stocks in all three size categories. Most funds specialize in only one size category. Therefore, the investor could own two or three funds in order to cover all the different size groups.

There are three other groups of stocks and mutual funds which are important. One is the growth group, the second is the value group of investments, and the third is a blend of growth and value. We'll call these the style groups, as opposed to the previous size groups. Certainly, the size groups and the style groups overlap each other. Figure 10-1 shows how they overlap.

Figure 10-1
Fund categories

Large-cap Growth	Large-cap Blend	Large-cap Value
Mid-cap Growth	Mid-cap Blend	Mid-cap Value
Small-cap Growth	Small-cap Blend	Small-cap Value

When the growth style is hot, the value style is often lackluster, and vice versa. Market psychology causes one group to be priced at more than its intrinsic value and another group at less than its intrinsic value. The problem is that these temporary cycles can last for years. Owners of stocks or funds in the "out-of-favor group" become discouraged after a long period of sub-par performance. However, it is important to remember that trends change. For instance, George has been holding a small-cap value fund for the last six years. During that time, Martha's large-cap growth fund has been outstanding. In contrast, his fund has done so poorly that he would have been better off in bonds or CDs. George feels terrible about his decision to hold the poor performing fund. Finally, after finishing their annual tax return and looking over their investments, George admits to Martha: "I really thought I could do better with my investments than you could do with yours. I have thought that risk taking is a good thing because the risk takers get rich while the others just get by. Yet, my riskier small stock value fund has been such a disappointment. I'm holding back the overall performance of our combined portfolio. I guess the financial writers have it right about large, growing companies being able to expand rapidly overseas. The small companies just can't compete against that. I'm exchanging my entire holding into additional shares of your large-cap growth fund. I don't know if it's the best thing, but it will certainly reduce my frustration."

Is George working from an emotional or a rational standpoint? You could say he's rational because he surely wants to end poor performance and achieve high performance. But really, his decision is more emotional than rational. He's embarrassed about having made what he now thinks was a mistake. He's been in a position of being "wrong" for several years now. It's uncomfortable for him to feel that he's been wrong. He wants to feel better. Truly, it is so easy to let emotions dictate or highly influence our investment choices.

When George completes the exchange, all of George and Martha's investments will be in a single style. The way to reduce risk is to be invested in both the growth and value styles or a blend of the two styles. George's action will increase the risk in the combined portfolio. Will George's action likely increase the total performance? Maybe yes; maybe no. Trends change. The possibility that the current trend has just about run its course is highly probable. At this point, the large-cap growth funds may be overpriced and the small-cap value funds may be poised to produce superior performance.

Certainly, it's not necessary to invest in all nine quadrants of Figure 10-1 to be well diversified; a total of two or three does a good job of reducing total risk.

Asset Allocation Formulas

Asset allocation is more art than science. Yet it can also get rather technical in terms of matching asset classes to each other and matching the total portfolio to the individual investor. The closer you get to retirement, the more important it is to get some professional individualized planning. At any age, don't put much credence in the "one size fits all" asset allocation recommendation. You may read that due to current market conditions an investment firm has changed its recommended allocation from 70% stocks, 20% bonds, 10% cash to 50% stocks, 30% bonds, 20% cash. These blanket recommendations ignore age, goals, and risk tolerance level. You need an allocation tailored to your individual situation.

Obviously, there is no single optimum allocation formula for each and every person reading this book. The best you can expect are some guidelines to get started. This book assumes that you want to accumulate a large amount of money, perhaps $1,000,000 or more. It also assumes that you can save some money, but you don't have a whole lot to invest each year. The most you can save annually is between $1,000 and $10,000. Under these circumstances, you should have a medium or high risk tolerance level. With a low risk tolerance level, it is very difficult to accomplish the goal of accumulating $1,000,000.

The most important advice I have for you is to start your savings and investment program NOW. That's more important than optimum investment allocation or anything else I can tell you.

I've said it before and I'll continue to say it: history is not bound to repeat itself. However, we can use history as a guide to make some recommendations. If you have a moderate or higher risk tolerance level and at least 20 years before needing the money, invest as much as 100% of your money in stock funds. When you get within 10 years of needing to withdraw money from your account, you should begin shifting to more conservative investments. By the time you reach retirement, at least 25% of your portfolio should be in intermediate-term bonds or other non stock investments.

If you have a relatively low risk tolerance and 20 or more years to reach your goal, invest in a balanced fund. As an alternative, you could invest some money into an equity-income fund and the rest into a bond fund. Investing 40% to 50% in a stock fund and the balance in a bond fund would be reasonable. The most conservative investors should put most of their money into intermediate-term government bonds. I recommend that these investors, who have at least twenty years to reach their goals, allocate no more than 20 percent of their long-term investments to money market assets, including CDs, T-bills, and GICs. As these investors come within ten years of needing to withdraw money, that percentage could increase gradually. Even the most conservative investors should have some funds allocated to stocks. In terms of investment style, the low risk investor should choose a stock fund managed in the value style, while the higher risk investor can go for either the growth or value style of portfolio management. Get started with a single mutual fund. After several years when your portfolio is larger, add another fund to achieve more diversification and hopefully improve your overall risk/return results.

If your risk tolerance level is extremely low, try to stretch a little bit outside of your comfort zone. Perhaps you've never thought that the stock market was safe. OK. Don't plunge head first into stock funds. However, I would encourage you to put at least 10% of your money into a stock fund or a balanced fund. Even the most conservative investors should keep at least 10% in stocks. The extremely risk-averse investor can build up to 10% or 20% in stocks by reinvesting the earnings from bond or money market investments into a stock or balanced fund. That way, the out-of-pocket principal will not be lost.

Asset allocation, as described above, is like getting fitted for a suit of clothes. The tailor measures you in terms of your inclination to take risk. The tailor then fits you with those investments which correspond to your risk profile.

Reaching Goals

Another method of asset allocation is to select a portfolio of investments based on its expected ability to meet your goals. How much money do you need? You need to ask yourself: what is my goal in money terms, how much can I invest, and how much time do I have to reach the goal? We'll assume that your long term savings program will consist of roughly equal installments made at least annually to an IRA or 401(k) plan.

Obviously, the rate of return is critical in the calculation of what you'll have at the end of your accumulation period, but other factors are also essential. The five variables in this investment equation are as follows:

1. How much money can you save and invest each year?
2. How many years will you save this money?
3. What is the rate of return you can earn on your investments?
4. How much risk are you willing to take on in your investment program?
5. How much money do you need to accumulate to reach your goal?

As you have learned from the previous chapter, risk and return are directly related. For the most part, if one goes up, the other also increases, and vice versa. Therefore, risk and return are treated as a single variable.

The other three variables of the equation are completely independent of each other. Since risk and return are considered a single variable, there are now four variables in this investment equation. The investment equation for this purpose can be summarized with the acronym NART. NUMBER of years, ANNUAL amount invested, at RATE of return (risk) equals TOTAL ending amount. Are any of these variables fixed or unchangeable in your particular circumstance?

Number of years

The number of years may appear to be fixed at first glance. However, this figure does have some variability. If you're 25 and your goal is to be accomplished at age 60, you have 35 years, right? Thirty-five years is the starting point for N (Number of years). With an excellent rate of return, you may be able to achieve your goal in 25 or 30 years, rather than 35 years. On the other hand, if your goal is $1,000,000, but you accumulated only $840,000 at age 60, you might decide to keep the account fully invested until age 63. With no additional out-of-pocket expenses, three additional years at 6% compounded growth increases the $840,000 to $1,000,453.

You're probably curious about why I just used an example of 6% growth between ages 60 and 63. In prior chapters, the examples assumed 10% and 12% growth. The reason is that in prior chapters the time frame was long-term. In this example, the updated time frame at age 60 is only three years, which is short-term. In order to achieve high assurance of reaching the goal in a short time, risk must be reduced. The lower risk investments tend to produce a lower return.

As we've seen, N is somewhat flexible at the end of the period. Yet, after such a long period of time has elapsed, you may not be willing or able to extend the time period for very much longer. For most people, N is more fixed than it is flexible at the end of the period.

For young people in their 20s or 30s, N appears to be quite flexible at the beginning of the period. Certainly it seems so to George. "Look, now is the time to enjoy life. It's certainly not the time to squirrel away money like some miser or something. When I settle down, when I get established in my career, then I'll be ready to save some money. Right now, I need spending money to have a good life. Since I don't make all that much, it's just too ridiculous to save anything. I'll start saving after a few more years. No big deal. For the next five years I wouldn't be able to save much anyway. So I'm going to have fun while I'm still young."

At age 25, George sees N as extremely flexible. If he waits until he's 30, he'll probably think he can wait another five years until he's 35. At age 35, he still has what seems like an eternity until age 62. Therefore, he decides to wait until he's 40 to start saving. As we showed earlier in the book, even a five or ten year delay can make an enormous difference in the total ending amount. Assuming an annual investment of $2000 earning a 12% compound return, a delay from age 25 to age 40 reduces the total amount at age 62 from $1,217,671 to $207,206. George's delay saved him $30,000 in contributions but cost him $1,010,465 in ending results!

Certainly, now is the time for George to enjoy life. Age 62 is also the time for George to enjoy the best of what life offers. With a little bit of balance and compromise, George can have it all. A small amount of annual savings won't cripple his lifestyle. Beginning early enough, it can produce a huge result. If the goal or total amount is substantial and the annual resources to reach the goal are modest, then N is not at all flexible at the beginning of the period. N must start now. Pay yourself first, and what is most important, do it now.

Annual amount

The Amount is not necessarily fixed. Let's assume your annual total spendable income is $15,000. If you pay yourself first $1000, you'll spend the other $14,000 on living expenses. If you save $2000, your other expenses will have to be $13,000. Your least important living expenses automatically reduce to the level where your total income minus your savings equals what you have left for living expenses. Therefore, the amount you save can change. Within reason, whatever amount you decide to pay yourself first is the amount you will save and invest.

From a practical standpoint, most people have an upper limit on what they can save. If you're at that limit now, it's unreasonable and probably a mistake to try to save any more. If you're already saving more than 10% to 20% of your income and you're already driving a used car and sharing your housing expenses, it's not reasonable for most people to save any more than that. For most people, that would be an upper limit. Of course, many people will have an upper limit for saving at less than 10% of their income.

Once again from a realistic standpoint, an upper limit for many people is the maximum amount the employer will match in their 401(k) plan, or $2000 in an IRA plan. Some other people will be able to contribute the maximum amount to their 401(k), even though the employer matches only a portion of that amount. In either case, unless you are particularly well off, your upper limit of savings is the maximum amount you can put in your 401(k) or IRA. Additional savings over and above that amount will not enjoy all the tax benefits you get in the above retirement plans. Understandably, most people are not going to increase their savings any further without the incentive of substantial tax savings and tax deferral. It's the tax savings and tax deferral that help make the total ending amount so large. Therefore, for most people, Number of years and Amount are somewhat flexible, but mostly fixed.

There are some people who do save more than the maximum allowable in their 401(k) and IRA plans. These people might invest the additional savings in tax deferred annuities, real estate, or other investments. This book can be very beneficial to people of all income levels; however, for information about savings and investing more than the maximum 401(k) and IRA annual limits, the reader will have to go to additional sources of information for help. There are other books to help these people, and there are many financial advisors available to work with them.

Rate of return

The Rate of return on your investments also has some elements of both flexibility and rigidity. If the number of years and the amount to invest are both rigid, then the way to reach your goal is to be flexible with the risk/return variable. If you need only 5% or 6% annual return to reach your goal, then your asset allocation will be primarily composed of money market funds and bond funds. If you need 7% to 9%, your asset allocation could be 100% in balanced funds. If you need more than 12% annual return, your assets should be allocated to aggressive growth funds and small-cap funds. Using this approach, you take on only as much risk as you need to in order to reach your goal. Perhaps your personal risk profile would allow you to take on more risk. But why do it? After all, why take on more risk than you need to. Looked at from this perspective, a flexible approach to risk/return seems to make good sense. The problem is that in the real world of capital accumulation, almost nobody can reach their goal with low risk/return investments.

If you can reach your goal with low return investments, the goal is probably too low. In order to reach a goal of $1,000,000 or more with only modest annual investments, you'll need to be invested, at least partially, in the stock market for a long period of time. Asset allocation entirely in CDs and bonds will not get the job done. Therefore, there is limited flexibility on the low side of the range of investment returns.

On the high side of investment returns, there is also limited flexibility. Once 100% of your assets are allocated to stock funds, there is only a little difference in returns between the most aggressive stock funds and the conservative stock funds. The risk among the different varieties of stock funds varies much more than the returns do. You can have a large increase in risk but only a small increase in return (if any increase at all) within the various categories of stock funds. Additionally, there is limited flexibility in the amount of risk a person can comfortably take. We've already discussed the emotional factor. If you worry too much and you can't sleep with high risk investments, you're not going to continue to hold on to them. Given a choice between meeting your goal and sleeping at night, you're going to sleep. The high risk investments will have to go, and the goal will be adjusted accordingly.

It is my hope that the insights and understanding gained from reading this book will enable many readers to take on slightly more risk. Hopefully, many readers will be willing to move at least some of their assets from CDs into stock funds or balanced funds. Yet, people can only change so much. I don't advise anyone to make radical changes in their risk tolerance. Radical changes won't last. Do it gradually and see how it works out with a small percentage of your assets in order to gain increased comfort and confidence.

Total amount

In terms of reaching your goal, we have looked at the three determining variables – Number of years, Amount, and Rate of return. The fourth factor (Total) is also variable. Those who start saving late in life come to realize that the $1,000,000 goal will not happen for them. The goal is very flexible downward for too many people. Obviously, you can offset a decline in one of the factors with an increase in another factor. For instance, you can offset a decline in the rate of return with an increased amount of annual investment. You can offset a decrease in number of years with an increase in the rate of return, etc. Certainly, you could even increase both of the other variables to offset a decline in the third variable. For instance, you could increase both the Amount and the Return to offset a reduced Number of years. Surely increasing all the other factors will make up for a late start. For example, if you delay starting a saving program until you're 40, you hope you can make up for it by salting away $6000 each year instead of $2000 and by increasing your return from 12% to 14%.

However, such a plan is far easier said than done. If you can't save $2000 now, how will you be able to save $6000 later? Your income may increase later, but so too will your spending. You'll be living in a more expensive residence, and most of your expenses will automatically increase to equal your income. That's just how life works! You spend what you make.

You will also have a problem in increasing the return on your investments. To increase your rate of return, you will have to take on substantially more risk. Once again, far easier said than done. The rate of return and amount to invest are not nearly as flexible as we want to believe. From a long-term historical standpoint, a 14% annual return is not realistic.

Even if you could put away $6000 each year for 22 years at 14% return, you would accumulate $823,782. If you had started a program at age 25, you would have done far better. $2000 per year for 37 years at 12% return produces a total of $1,217,671. The sooner you start investing, the more realistic your chances are of obtaining your goal.

In summary, there are two basic approaches to asset allocation. One approach is to match investment risks with your personal risk profile. But remember, the rate of return may be too low to reach your goal if you have low risk tolerance. You may have to settle for a lesser goal.

The other approach is to calculate what rate of return you need to earn to reach the goal. Then allocate assets to those investments which historically have provided the required return. One problem is that the required rate of return may be so high that it's simply unattainable. The other problem is that the required rate of return may require investments which are too far out of your comfort zone. You can't handle the risk.

The best approach for some people may be a combination approach. Start off with the first approach. Choose a fund with the level of risk you are comfortable with and then calculate your expected ending total amount. (See Appendix D for instructions on how to make the calculations.) If the ending amount is lower than your goal, choose one additional fund. The second fund should be a stock fund, although not an aggressive stock fund. Allocate 80% of your assets to the fund you are comfortable with and 20% of your assets to the stock fund. Any more than 20% is probably too far out of your comfort zone.

When making your calculations, keep in mind that history is not bound to repeat itself. The stock fund which historically produced a return of 12% may produce substantially more or less than 12% in the future. Since we aren't certain of the future rate of return, we can't be certain of the ending total amount. Therefore, save what you can, allocate it according to your risk profile, and hope for the best.

Conclusion

Asset allocation is not exact science. Therefore, there are no perfect answers to the asset allocation question. Based on your risk profile and goals, allocate between 20% and 100% to stock funds. You can always make asset allocation adjustments later. However, starting your investment program later is the one thing you can't afford to do.

THE TIME TO START IS NOW

CHAPTER 11

MUTUAL FUND SELECTION

Making a good mutual fund selection can be a daunting task. But it doesn't have to be so difficult. In this chapter, I'll discuss the complications of fund selection, and then I'll show you how to cut through those complications and make some easy choices.

Perhaps the worst aspect of fund selection is that you may not know for months, or even years, whether or not you made a good selection. If you buy a computer, a car, or an appliance, you'll know rather quickly whether or not you got a lemon. With a mutual fund, you're not buying current benefits. You're buying future benefits. How well will your fund do in the future? Without a crystal ball, you don't know. You can't make your decision in the future. You have to rely on information from the past and the present.

Instead of beginning with the entire universe of funds, I'll focus on those funds which are appropriate for you. Later, I'll explain how to quickly weed out most funds to leave you with a short list for more detailed review.

Fund Categories

First, you want to look at the category or categories of funds which are appropriate for you, as discussed in the chapters on risk and asset allocation. I'm assuming your goal is capital appreciation and your time frame is long-term. Consider this ranking of categories as a general guideline only. Some individual funds may be more or less risky than their category would indicate. For instance, some funds in the growth & income category may be more risky than some aggressive growth funds.

The following chart outlines my general recommendations

You risk tolerance	Appropriate categories
Extremely low	Money market funds
	Intermediate-term bond funds
Low	Long-term bond funds
	Balanced funds
Moderate	Equity-income funds
	Growth & income funds
	Growth funds
	Global funds
High	Aggressive growth funds
	Small-cap funds
	Sector funds
	International funds

A significant category of stock funds is not included in the above list. In looking at the historical risk/return results of mutual funds, one category stands out like a sore thumb. Gold/precious metals funds over long term time periods have had the lowest returns and highest risks of all the major categories of stock funds. In a few periods, these funds have done extremely well. However, gold funds should never be more than a small portion of any long term portfolio. Most investors should totally avoid this category.

If your risk tolerance level is high, you can invest in any of the categories, even those with low risk. At times, even money market funds or bond funds may be appropriate for high risk investors. The reverse is not true. Aggressive and small-cap funds are never appropriate for those with extremely low risk tolerance.

Investment objective vs. investment style

It's easy to get investment style categories confused with investment objective categories. Even some of the reporting services lump investment objectives and investment styles together. The investment objective is what the fund wants to do. The fund wants to produce aggressive growth, growth, income, or growth & income. These investment objectives are the most basic fund categories. There are additional investment objective categories, which are actually subcategories of the above four categories. For instance, there are gold funds and other sector funds. Such funds are actually specialized aggressive growth funds. Balanced funds and equity-income funds are actually subcategories of funds with the investment objective of producing growth & income.

Style categories refer to the nine types of stock funds as described in the previous chapter. These types refer to the size of the company (small, mid, large) and whether the stock is growth, value, or a blend of growth and value.

Some financial publications overlap fund styles and fund categories. Don't become frustrated or confused with the lack of uniformity or preciseness of styles and categories. What's more important is to evaluate individual funds to see which one or ones have the best risk/reward probabilities for you.

Past Performance

Past performance is probably the most obvious starting point in selecting a fund. In the absence of substantial changes, poor performing funds would be expected to do poorly in the future. The research indicates that, indeed, most funds in the bottom 20% of their categories continue to perform below average in the future. So, definitely avoid the worst performing funds. The law of averages does not come back around to benefit these funds, generally speaking. On the other hand, the research indicates that good past performance is not a highly reliable predictor of future performance. You simply can't select the funds that performed in the top 10%

over the last three or five years and be entirely comfortable that they will be in the top 10% three or five years from now. Nevertheless, past performance does offer some evidence of the competency of fund managers.

Comparing apples to apples

It is important in comparing funds to compare a fund to its category rather than to all funds. For instance, a small-cap growth fund should be compared to small-cap growth funds only. It should not be compared to all stock funds. You want to hold a fund that is performing well in comparison to its peers.

Continuity of management

Some mutual funds have a high turnover of fund managers. High turnover of managers is one obvious reason that good past performance doesn't always result in good future performance for a fund. When an outstanding star manager leaves one fund and goes to another fund, the performance of the first fund often suffers. So, when evaluating fund performance, determine how long the current manager has been managing that fund. Such management information is reported in the fund's prospectus. It is also reported in trade publications, such as Morningstar.

The mutual fund industry is highly competitive. All funds want to be ranked in the top half or top quarter or even first in their category. Such information is readily available to the public. It's kind of like the race to the Super Bowl or any other sports championship. The coaches whose teams make the playoffs usually get retained, while coaches of losing teams often get the ax. Similarly, portfolio managers of well performing funds are highly valued by their management companies. The trick is to prevent other firms from hiring away those top managers. As in nearly all aspects of analyzing mutual funds, nothing is guaranteed. Even the best managers go through dry spells of below average performance.

As stated earlier, not all funds are managed by a single manager who is solely responsible for the investment buy and sell decisions. Some funds use the "committee" system of investment management.

In the committee system, a team of professionals makes the decisions. The management corporation believes the team provides continuity and the departure of a single member of the team is not important. Nevertheless, continuity of management is important. Continuity of the star or continuity of the committee is an important consideration.

Consistency of performance

Investors with low risk tolerance need consistency of performance. With consistency, the losses during market downturns are minimized. The modest losses during down periods offset only a small portion of the gains during up periods in the market. Fans of consistency like to present the example of two funds gaining the same net percentage over a two-year period. For example, both Fund A and Fund B gain a net 20% over two years. Fund A gains 25% in year one, followed by a 5% loss in year two. Net is (+25% -5%) = 20%. Fund B gains 50% in year one followed by a 30% drop in year two. Net is (+50% - 30%) = 20%. If $1000 is invested in each fund at the beginning of year one, Fund A's ending value is $1187.50, while Fund B's ending value is $1050. Looked at from this theoretical perspective, consistency produces superior results. In the real world, however, consistency generally doesn't produce the best long-term results. However, it does allow low risk investors to sleep at night. Without consistency, low risk investors would be very reluctant to put any money in the stock market. What low risk investors need is a stock or a balanced mutual fund which provides consistency of performance.

Good consistent performance exists, but it is rare. Of course, there's no guarantee that funds achieving such good, consistent performance for the prior 10 years can do it again in the next 10 years. The volatility of a given fund will increase or decrease along with the overall market. But the relative risk level of different funds tends to remain about the same. Balanced funds tend to stay less volatile than equity-income and growth & income funds. In turn, the equity-income and growth & income funds stay less risky than growth funds. Aggressive growth funds and small-cap funds will almost always have the wildest up and down rides.

Risk-Adjusted Performance

For those investors who can tolerate moderate to high risk, there exists the potential for long term gains significantly greater than the overall market. In practice, this means that the high performance funds lose as much or more than the overall market during downturns. Nevertheless, given equal performance, less risk is better than more risk.

Risk-adjusted performance (previously covered in more detail in Chapter 9) is rather technical and complex. In order to make this understandable, I'll try to keep the discussion as simple as possible.

There are three measures of risk-adjusted performance: the Sharpe Index, the Treynor Index, and "alpha." In comparing one fund to another, the fund with the higher Sharpe or Treynor Index number is the better risk-adjusted fund. The alpha indicates how much better or worse a fund performed than it was expected to perform, given the amount of risk. An alpha of 0.00 indicates that the fund performed no better or worse than the average fund with equal risk. Look for funds with positive alphas, the higher the better. Some mutual fund rating services provide one or the other of these indexes or ratios as they are sometimes referred to.

Fund Expenses

All mutual fund investors should consider the fees and charges associated with particular funds they are interested in. Fees and charges are detailed near the beginning of each fund's prospectus. On Fridays, "The Wall Street Journal" provides each fund's annual expense ratio in the mutual fund tables. The Wall Street Journal also provides footnotes indicating which funds are load funds and which are no-load. Several other mutual fund services also provide this information.

As with performance, compare expenses of funds in the same category. Generally speaking, the riskier the category the higher the expense ratio is. Balanced funds, equity-income funds, and growth & income funds have lower average expense ratios that growth funds, small-cap funds, and international funds.

Fund supermarkets like Charles Schwab and Fidelity offer investors hundreds of no-load funds to choose from. It's a nice convenience for the investor. There are no transaction fees in many cases. However, many funds not included in the supermarkets have lower expense ratios than do funds included in the supermarkets. Therefore, don't limit your selection only to those funds in the supermarket.

Load Funds

Load funds are a good choice for some investors. The sales charges compensate the broker for financial planning and fund selection services. Most financial writers have a bias toward no-load funds. These writers don't need the services of a broker or financial planner and they think you can do without those services too. Just read the information offered and save big on sales expenses! It does sound like a good strategy for everyone to save on sales charges. However, the financial writers cannot give advice for unique situations in their articles and books, nor can they give you a personalized and comprehensive financial plan. Some people don't have the time to do their own planning. Some others have complex needs requiring personalized expert counseling. If you need personal help, load funds sold by a knowledgeable broker may be right for you. If you don't need these services, don't buy load funds.

The studies I've seen indicate that load and no-load funds perform approximately the same on average, before sales charges are taken into account. Factor in the load, and the advantage clearly goes to the no-load fund. So, if you don't need financial planning or fund selection services, no-load funds are definitely better. You can buy no-load funds directly from the fund company. Their toll-free telephone numbers are readily available in the reporting services. The quarterly mutual funds report in "The Wall Street Journal" also provides the telephone numbers.

If you do need the services of a broker or financial planner, be aware that there is a very wide range of expertise and a wide range of expenses. Higher expenses don't necessarily mean more expertise. It used to be easy to understand the expenses associated with load funds. It's now rather complex.

Until recently, there was only a single class of load funds. These funds, front-end load funds, are now sometimes called Class A funds. They have the sales charges built into the purchasing price of the shares. In the mid 1980s brokerage firms created a two tiered system. The alternative to Class A shares was Class B shares, which had no up-front charges but had gradually declining redemption charges over a five to seven-year period. Of course, if the investor held the shares for longer than the seven years, the broker didn't go hungry! The Class B shares have 12b-1 distribution fees which are usually 1.0% annually. The broker gets compensated from the 12b-1 fees. Be aware that in some cases, the 12b-1 fees reduce from 1.0% to 0.25% or less after several years. In other cases the 12b-1 fees continue indefinitely at 1.0% annually, and are often called level-load or Class C shares. Now there are Class C, Class D, Class 1, Class 2 and several other classes of shares. Unfortunately for investors, there are no standardized definitions.

The different share classes may have different prospectuses. So, you may not find out about all of the various load options by reading the prospectus or by asking the broker. Realize that when you get shares through a broker, you are paying the broker, either directly or indirectly. Your payment could show up as front-end sales charges, redemption fees, 12b-1 fees, or a combination of the above.

Financial planners using no-load funds

As an alternative to selling you load funds, a financial planner or broker may put you in no-load funds. In that case, the planner will still be compensated. Generally, the broker or planner charges his or her own annual fee, called a *wrap fee*. The wrap fee is usually 1.0% or more of the market value of the portfolio each year. The fee could be more or less than 1.0%, depending on the planner. A wrap fee may not seem like a whole lot, particularly when the market is going up. However, 1.0% each and every year is too much if you are able to do it yourself.

Fund Size

Fund size in this context means total assets of the mutual fund. For bond and money market funds, size merely affects fund operating expenses. Therefore, it is not necessary to consider size separately as a factor in evaluating bond and money market funds. The situation for stock funds is more complicated. The research data indicates that the best stock fund performers tend to be small size mutual funds – less than $300 million in total assets. However, the biggest losers also tend to be small funds. Therefore, if you want to reduce the risk of poor fund selection, large size is preferable to small.

Portfolio Turnover

High *portfolio turnover* means the fund sells most of its assets during the year, and uses that money to buy different securities. Low portfolio turnover means the fund uses a buy and hold strategy. In theory, high portfolio turnover is a drag on fund performance. It generates high transaction costs for the fund. However, I haven't seen any research to prove that mutual funds with high portfolio turnover have poorer performance as a result. There are enough other factors to consider in selecting a mutual fund. I don't believe this one justifies any additional time on the part of the investor.

Filter Funds With Multiple Criteria

There are more than six thousand stock oriented mutual funds (including international and balanced funds) out there for investors to look at. Yet, setting a few simple standards can reduce the number to a few dozen. If you're not using a broker, the first standard is to exclude all load funds, including low-load funds. Exclude all funds with high annual expenses, say all funds with expenses more than 1.4%. Exclude global funds, specialty funds, and funds with a high minimum investment amount, say $5000 or more. Then exclude any fund which didn't beat the performance of 60% of the funds in its category over the last three and five years. Finally, make sure the manager responsible for that performance is still on board. "The Wall Street Journal" on May 11, 1999 page C1 performed such a filtering process with the assistance of Morningstar. The ending list consisted of only 64 funds in several different categories. No doubt, a few of those 64 funds will perform worse than average in the future. Some funds not on the list will likely perform better than those on the list. However, the filtering technique is a very effective way to begin the fund selection process.

A few companies offer computer software so that you can filter funds on your own computer. These companies include Morningstar and Steele Systems, Inc. You can contact Morningstar at (800) 735-0700 and Steele Systems at (800) 379-0679. I have used only Steele's "Mutual Fund Expert™ ," and I like it. As with my other lists of suppliers, these are not the only companies offering the service.

The easiest way to filter funds is to use the rating services at your local library. The services most likely to be found at the library are Morningstar, CDA Weisenberger, and Value Line. Many investors use the star or ranking systems of these services to filter in, so to speak, the top risk-adjusted funds. These investors compare the top rated funds to each other and then invest in one or two of them. This technique is a reasonable and popular way to select funds.

When to sell

Now, let's say you invest in a fund which is highly rated by one of the above rating services. Several years from now that fund may not be performing very well. How do you know when to get out of that fund? First, it is important to state again that fund selection is more art than science. That being said, look at the criteria for choosing a fund and see if it still meets the criteria. Has the fund manager changed? If so, was the previous manager a "star" and is the new manager relatively inexperienced? If such is the case, you'll want to look at moving out of this particular fund. Next, evaluate recent performance with an apple to apples approach. Namely, compare a large-cap growth fund to the large-cap growth fund average, etc. Don't be too impatient. Changing funds on the basis of three months performance is too impatient. However, if your fund goes to the bottom half of its category for two years, it's time to get out.

If your risk tolerance level has changed, it's time to make a switch. If you're now within ten years of retirement, it may be time to make some changes in asset allocation. Doing it yourself can work well for many people in the early accumulation years. But when you get close to retirement, you should have a professional assist you in avoiding the problem of running out of money prematurely.

Index Funds

Indexes measure the performance of a group of stocks or bonds. As such, indexes are a popular gauge as to how well various mutual funds are performing. If a mutual fund performs better than the appropriate index, then the fund has been well managed. So indexes give investors another benchmark with which to compare their results. Experienced investors are well aware of the Dow Jones Industrial Average (DJIA) and the Standard & Poor's 500 Composite Stock Price Index (S&P 500). The DJIA is a very narrow index because it takes into account only 30 stocks. The stocks are large-cap "blue chip" companies. The S&P 500 also comprises large-cap blue chip companies, 500 of them. The S&P

500 accounts for approximately two-thirds of the U.S. stock market value.

The S&P 500 Index is made up of both value stocks and growth stocks. Standard & Poor's Corporation (S&P) and BARRA Associates divided the S&P 500 into two indexes. One is the Value Index and the other is the Growth Index.

There are many other indexes. Some are well known and others not so well known. The Wilshire 5000 Index represents all regularly traded U.S. common stocks. The Wilshire 4500 Index, a portion of the Wilshire 5000, excludes those stocks in the S&P 500 Index. Consequently, the Wilshire 4500 would be a benchmark for funds investing in small-cap and mid-cap stocks. The Russell 2000 Index is the most widely accepted benchmark for U.S. small-cap stocks. There are also international stock indexes. Bonds have not been left out of all indexes. The Lehman Brothers Aggregate Bond Index represents the entire U.S. taxable bond market, including U.S. Treasury and government agency securities, mortgage-backed issues, and high and medium quality corporate bonds.

Now there are mutual funds which seek to match the performance of various indexes. The fund manager attempts to replicate the investment results of the index by holding either all of the securities or a large sample of the securities in the index. There is no attempt to beat the index by investing mostly in the manager's favorite stocks. Managing an index fund is a "passive" investment approach emphasizing broad diversification and low portfolio turnover. The fund's investment policies and restrictions are precisely defined and easy to understand. The portfolio managers of index funds have very strict policies requiring them to match the index. Thus, the index funds are more predictable than regular, managed funds. By definition, the index fund should perform about the same as the index less the index fund's expense ratio.

The major advantage of index funds is significantly lower expenses than standard, managed funds. The expense ratios for most common stock mutual funds range from 1.00% to 2.00%, while index fund expenses usually range between 0.20% and 0.50%.

On average, over long periods, index funds and managed funds tend to have approximately the same performance before expenses. After subtracting lower expenses, the index fund is at an advantage in comparison to the average managed fund. In most historical periods, index funds have enjoyed better net performance than most managed funds.

Despite the long-term average results, there are always some managed funds which beat the index funds. Be aware that there are also some managed funds which substantially under perform the index funds. Those managed funds which beat the indexes have managers who have made particularly good investment decisions in the past. Investors in regular, managed funds believe they can select those particular funds which will make similarly excellent investment decisions in the future. Some mutual fund investors are successful in picking superior managed funds but most are not. Investors should realize that it takes time to study and analyze actively managed funds. Excellent fund selection is an art, as well as a science.

If you don't have the time to study managed mutual funds or don't have an expert to help you, index funds are a good choice. Many people who do have the time to analyze funds prefer index funds for reasons stated above – low expenses and strict investment policies. For most investors, index funds are an excellent choice. Nevertheless, there is no perfectly correct answer as to whether an index fund is better or worse than an actively managed fund.

There are several indexes which have related index funds. Which index will you choose to match with an index fund? The several indexes may produce substantially different results. Some indexes could actually go up while others go down. The problem is that you might choose the worst performing index. Even if you avoid the difficult choice of choosing an actively managed fund, you still have to choose an index to invest in. There's no perfect answer to this question. Most investors will do just fine tracking the Wilshire 5000 Index or the S&P 500 Index. These two indexes are well diversified. Historically, most investors have used the S&P 500 Index with excellent results. Investors who want part of their total portfolio in a higher risk index can allocate a portion of their money into a small-cap index, such as the Russell 2000 Index. To invest in an index fund, call a mutual fund company and tell the representative to send you a prospectus of their index fund which tracks one of the above-mentioned indexes. The representative can also answer any of your questions about their funds and send forms so you can set up a tax-deferred retirement account.

In my opinion, a good index fund has an expense ratio of 0.50% or less. Numerous fund groups have index funds which meet that criterion. The best index funds are those which come closest to matching the historical performance of the related index. Those funds typically have the lowest expense ratios. Index funds provide these performance and expense numbers to you in the literature they send you upon request. I mention three groups here, all of which have excellent index funds. All three of these companies also have several excellent managed mutual funds. Vanguard has been the leader in index funds and has the greatest number of such funds. The telephone numbers and Internet addresses of these companies are as follows:

Fidelity	(800) 544-6666	www.fidelity.com
T. Rowe Price	(800) 225-5132	www.troweprice.com
Vanguard	(800) 635-1511	www.vanguard.com

Those of you who are interested in beating the indexes should do additional research on managed funds after reading this book. Although the above three companies do have some excellent managed funds, I recommend that you not limit your research to those three companies for your IRA or 401(k).

Conclusion

The following are general guidelines for most people. If you're in your 20s or 30s and have a moderate or high risk tolerance level, put all your IRA and 401(k) money into stock funds. If you're in your 40s, 50s, or 60s, at least some of your money should be in stock funds. Index funds can be a good choice for most investors.

Remember that an employer 401(k) plan with matching contributions is like an offer to increase your pay. If you pay yourself first, it's not too hard to make your contribution to the plan. You can't afford not to make the contribution. Start your 401(k) and /or IRA today, and give yourself the chance to:

Become a Millionaire in Your Current Job.

Appendix A

Hypothetical investment of $1000 per year into CDs. This example assumes the CD earns 6% and the stock fund earns 12%, both compounded annually. The CD only column assumes all income is reinvested in CDs. The combination total amount assumes all income is reinvested into a stock mutual fund.

| Year-end | CD Only | Combination of CD and Stock Fund | | |
		CD	+ Stock Fund	Total Amount
1	$ 1,060	$ 1,000	$ 60	$ 1,060
2	2,184	2,000	187	2,187
3	3,375	3,000	389	3,389
4	4,637	4,000	676	4,676
5	5,975	5,000	1,057	6,057
6	7,393	6,000	1,544	7,544
7	8,897	7,000	2,149	9,149
8	10,491	8,000	2,887	10,887
9	12,180	9,000	3,773	12,773
10	13,971	10,000	4,826	14,826
11	15,869	11,000	6,065	17,065
12	17,882	12,000	7,513	19,513
13	20,015	13,000	9,195	23,195
14	22,276	14,000	11,138	25,138
15	24,672	15,000	13,775	28,375
16	27,212	16,000	16,388	32,388
17	29,905	17,000	19,375	36,375
18	32,759	18,000	22,780	40,780
19	35,785	19,000	26,654	45,654
20	38,992	20,000	31,052	51,052
21	42,391	21,000	36,038	57,038
22	45,995	22,000	41,683	63,683
23	49,814	23,000	48,065	71,065
24	53,863	24,000	55,273	79,273
25	$ 58,155	$ 25,000	$ 63,406	$ 88,406

Appendix B

Annual Investment Required to Meet Future Lump Sum Goal
Explanations and assumptions follow Line 8 below.

Line 1   Today's cost of your goal $100,000

Line 2   Estimated annual rate of inflation of your goal
         between now and target date   3%

Line 3   Number of years between now and target date   15

Line 4   Factor in "Growth of $1" table (Page 188)   1.5580
         (Based on lines 2 and 3)

Line 5   Estimated future cost of goal $155,800
         (Multiply Line 1 times Line 5)

Line 6   Estimated rate of growth in investments   9%

Line 7   Factor in "Savings growth" table (Page 189)   32.0034
         (Based on Lines 3 and 6)

Line 8   Required annual investment contributions $4868
         (Line 5 divided by Line 7)

In the example above, you want to buy a boat in 15 years (Line 3). The current price of the kind of boat you want is $100,000 (Line 1). You've been going to boat shows for the last several years. Each year, you've noticed that the price of the boat goes up by around 3%. It's reasonable to assume that past rate of inflation will continue into the future. So, you estimate this type of boat will continue to increase in price about 3% (Line 2) each year for the next 15 years. Go to the Growth of $1 table in Appendix D. Under the 3% column across from 15 years, you'll see the factor 1.5580 (Line 4). Multiply $100,000 times 1.5580 to get $155,800 (Line 5). Line 6 depends on your asset allocation, which is a personal decision. Let's say your portfolio is 80% stocks and 20% bonds.

Large company stocks have gained about 11.0% compounded annually since 1926 and bonds have returned a bit more than 5%. You want to be conservative; so you estimate 10% return on the stock portion of your portfolio and 5% return on the bond portion. 80% in stocks times 10% return equals 8%, and 20% in bonds times 5% return equals 1%. Thus, the expected rate of return on the portfolio is: 8% + 1% equals 9% (Line 6). Next go to the Savings growth table in Appendix D. Under the 9% column across from 15 years, you'll see the factor 32.0034 (Line 7). Finally, divide Line 5 amount $155,800 by Line 7 factor 32.0034 to get $4868 (Line 8). $4868 is the required annual investment to reach your goal using the above assumptions on inflation and investment growth.

Appendix C

Formula for Calculating Estimated Cost of Car Ownership

1	Beginning mileage of the car	_____
2	Estimated (EST) ending mileage	_____
3	EST miles to be driven. Line 1 minus Line 2	_____
4	Miles per gallon for this car	_____
5	EST gallons of gas usage. Line 3 divided by Line 4	_____
6	EST cost of a gallon of gas	_____
7	Fuel expense. Line 5 times Line 6	_____
8	Month & year of car purchase	_____
9	EST month & year of car sale	_____
10	Number of months car ownership	_____
11	Monthly car insurance expense	_____
12	EST total car insurance expense. Line 10 times Line 11	_____
13	Monthly parking fees if any	_____
14	Total parking fees. Line 10 times Line 13	_____
15	Price of car including taxes & fees. See below	_____
16	EST cost of maintenance & repairs for mileage in Line 3	_____
17	EST trade-in value of the car at Line 9	_____
18	EST total cost of car ownership. Add lines 7,12,14,15,16	_____
19	EST net cost of car ownership. Line 18 minus Line 17	_____
20	EST cost per mile driven. Line 19 divided by Line 3	_____
15a	Down payment plus trade-in or cash price	_____
15b	Balance to finance	_____
15c	Monthly payment	_____
15d	Number of months to pay	_____
15e	Total monthly payments. Line 15c times Line 15d	_____
15f	Price of car including financing. Line 15a plus Line 15e	_____
	Enter Line 15f on Line 15 above	

Calculation of Cost of 1993 Car Purchased April 1996. Cash Basis

1	Beginning mileage of the car	36,000
2	Estimated (EST) ending mileage	144,000
3	EST miles to be driven. Line 1 minus Line 2	108,000
4	Miles per gallon for this car	20
5	EST gallons of gas usage. Line 3 divided by Line 4	5,400
6	EST cost of a gallon of gas	$1.25
7	Fuel expense. Line 5 times Line 6	$6,750
8	Month & year of car purchase	04/1996
9	EST month & year of car sale	04/2005
10	Number of months car ownership	108
11	Monthly car insurance expense	$75
12	EST total car insurance expense. Line 10 times Line 11	$8,100
13	Monthly parking fees if any	-0-
14	Total parking fees. Line 10 times Line 13	-0-
15	Price of car including taxes & fees. See below	$8,500
16	EST cost of maintenance & repairs for mileage in Line 3	$6,000
17	EST trade-in value of the car at Line 9	$800
18	EST total cost of car ownership. Add lines 7,12,14,15,16	$29,350
19	EST net cost of car ownership. Line 18 minus Line 17	$28,550
20	EST cost per mile driven. Line 19 divided by Line 3	26 cents
15a	Down payment plus trade-in or cash price	$8,500
15b	Balance to finance	
15c	Monthly payment	
15d	Number of months to pay	
15e	Total monthly payments. Line 15c times Line 15d	
15f	Price of car including financing. Line 15a plus Line 15e	$8,500
	Enter Line 15f on Line 15 above	

Calculation of Cost of 1993 Car Purchased April 1996.
Financing for 36 Months at 9% Interest

1	Beginning mileage of the car	36,000
2	Estimated (EST) ending mileage	144,000
3	EST miles to be driven. Line 1 minus Line 2	108,000
4	Miles per gallon for this car	20
5	EST gallons of gas usage. Line 3 divided by Line 4	5,400
6	EST cost of a gallon of gas	$1.25
7	Fuel expense. Line 5 times Line 6	$6,750
8	Month & year of car purchase	04/1996
9	EST month & year of car sale	04/2005
10	Number of months car ownership	108
11	Monthly car insurance expense	$75
12	EST total car insurance expense. Line 10 times Line 11	$8,100
13	Monthly parking fees if any	-0-
14	Total parking fees. Line 10 times Line 13	-0-
15	Price of car including taxes & fees. See below	$9,528
16	EST cost of maintenance & repairs for mileage in Line 3	$6,000
17	EST trade-in value of the car at Line 9	$800
18	EST total cost of car ownership. Add lines 7,12,14,15,16	$30,378
19	EST net cost of car ownership. Line 18 minus Line 17	$59,578
20	EST cost per mile driven. Line 19 divided by Line 3	27 cents
15a	Down payment plus trade-in or cash price	$1,500
15b	Balance to finance	$7,000
15c	Monthly payment	$223
15d	Number of months to pay	36
15e	Total monthly payments. Line 15c times Line 15d	$8,028
15f	Price of car including financing. Line 15a plus Line 15e	$9,528
	Enter Line 15f on Line 15 above	

Calculation of Costs of New Cars in 1996, 1999, and 2002
Cash Basis

	New car #1	New car #2	New car #3	Total
Line 1	-0-	-0-	-0-	-0-
Line 2	36,000	36,000	36,000	108,000
Line 3	36,000	36,000	36,000	108,000
Line 4	20	20	20	20
Line 5	1,800	1,800	1,800	5,400
Line 6	1.25	1.25	1.25	1.25
Line 7	2,250	2,250	2,250	6,750
Line 8	04/1996	04/1999	04/2002	
Line 9	04/1999	04/2002	04/2005	
Line 10	36	36	36	108
Line 11	$75	$75	$75	$75
Line 12	$2,700	$2,700	$2,700	$8,100
Line 13	-0-	-0-	-0-	-0-
Line 14	-0-	-0-	-0-	-0-
Line 15	$18,000	$20,000	$22,000	$60,000
Line 16	$700	$700	$700	$2,100
Line 17	$8,000	$9,000	$10,000	$27,000
Line 18	$23,650	$25,650	$28,150	$76,950
Line 19	$15,650	$16,650	$18,150	$49,950
Line 20	43 cents	46 cents	50 cents	46 cents

Calculation of Costs on New Cars in 1996, 1999, and 2002
Financing Each Car for 36 Months at 9% Interest

	New car #1	New car #2	New car #3	Total
Line 1	-0-	-0-	-0-	-0-
Line 2	36,000	36,000	36,000	108,000
Line 3	36,000	36,000	36,000	108,000
Line 4	20	20	20	20
Line 5	1,800	1,800	1,800	5,400
Line 6	1.25	1.25	1.25	1.25
Line 7	2,250	2,250	2,250	6,750
Line 8	04/1996	04/1999	04/2002	
Line 9	04/1999	04/2002	04/2005	
Line 10	36	36	36	108
Line 11	$75	$75	$75	$75
Line 12	$2,700	$2,700	$2,700	$8,100
Line 13	-0-	-0-	-0-	-0-
Line 14	-0-	-0-	-0-	-0-
Line 15	$20,172	$21,752	$23,868	$65,792
Line 16	$700	$700	$700	$2,100
Line 17	$8,000	$9,000	$10,000	$27,000
Line 18	$25,822	$27,402	$29,518	$82,742
Line 19	$17,822	$18,402	$19,518	$55,742
Line 20	50 cents	51 cents	54 cents	52 cents
Line 15a	$3,000	$8,000	$9,000	$20,000
Line 15b	$15,000	$12,000	$13,000	$40,000
Line 15c	$477	$382	$413	
Line 15d	36	36	36	108
Line 15e	$17,172	$13,752	$14,868	$45,792
Line 15f	$20,172	$21,752	$23,868	$65,792

Appendix D

GROWTH OF $1

This table shows what a single $1 deposit will grow to in the future with annual compounding.

Year	1.00%	2.00%	3.00%	4.00%	5.00%	6.00%	7.00%
1	1.0100	1.0200	1.0300	1.0400	1.0500	1.0600	1.0700
2	1.0201	1.0404	1.0609	1.0816	1.1025	1.1236	1.1449
3	1.0303	1.0612	1.0927	1.1249	1.1576	1.1910	1.2250
4	1.0406	1.0824	1.1255	1.1699	1.2155	1.2625	1.3108
5	1.0510	1.1041	1.1593	1.2167	1.2763	1.3382	1.4026
6	1.0615	1.1262	1.1941	1.2653	1.3401	1.4185	1.5007
7	1.0721	1.1487	1.2299	1.3159	1.4071	1.5036	1.6058
8	1.0829	1.1717	1.2668	1.3686	1.4775	1.5938	1.7182
9	1.0937	1.1951	1.3048	1.4233	1.5513	1.6895	1.8385
10	1.1046	1.2190	1.3439	1.4802	1.6289	1.7908	1.9672
15	1.1610	1.3459	1.5580	1.8009	2.0789	2.3966	2.7590
20	1.2202	1.4859	1.8061	2.1911	2.6533	3.2071	3.8697
25	1.2824	1.6406	2.0938	2.6658	3.3864	4.2919	5.4274
30	1.3478	1.8114	2.4273	3.2434	4.3219	5.7435	7.6123
35	1.4166	2.0000	2.8139	3.9461	5.5160	7.6861	10.6766
40	1.4889	2.2080	3.2620	4.8010	7.0400	10.2857	14.9745
Year	8.00%	9.00%	10.00%	11.00%	12.00%	14.00%	15.00%
1	1.0800	1.0900	1.1000	1.1100	1.1200	1.1400	1.1500
2	1.1664	1.1881	1.2100	1.2321	1.2544	1.2996	1.3255
3	1.2597	1.2950	1.3310	1.3676	1.4049	1.4815	1.5209
4	1.3605	1.4116	1.4641	1.5181	1.5735	1.6890	1.7490
5	1.4693	1.5386	1.6105	1.6851	1.7623	1.9254	2.0114
6	1.5869	1.6771	1.7716	1.8704	1.9738	2.1950	2.3131
7	1.7138	1.8280	1.9487	2.0762	2.2107	2.5023	2.6600
8	1.8509	1.9926	2.1436	2.3045	2.4760	2.8526	3.0590
9	1.9990	2.1719	2.3579	2.5580	2.7731	3.2519	3.5179
10	2.1589	2.3674	2.5937	2.8394	3.1058	3.7072	4.0456
15	3.1722	3.6425	4.1772	4.7846	5.4736	7.1379	8.1371
20	4.6610	5.6044	6.7275	8.0623	9.6463	13.7435	16.3665
25	6.8485	8.6231	10.8347	13.5855	17.0001	26.4619	32.9190
30	10.0627	13.2677	17.4494	22.8923	29.9599	50.9502	66.2118
35	14.7853	20.4140	28.1024	38.5749	52.7996	98.1002	133.1755
40	21.7245	31.4094	45.2593	65.0001	93.0510	188.8835	267.8635

SAVINGS GROWTH
This table shows what a series of $1 deposits grow to in the future with annual compounding.

Year	1.00%	2.00%	3.00%	4.00%	5.00%	6.00%	7.00%
1	1.0100	1.0200	1.0300	1.0400	1.0500	1.0600	1.0700
2	2.0301	2.0604	2.0909	2.1216	2.1525	2.1836	2.2149
3	3.0604	3.1216	3.1836	3.2465	3.3101	3.3746	3.4399
4	4.1010	4.2040	4.3091	4.4163	4.5256	4.6371	4.7507
5	5.1520	5.3081	5.4684	5.6330	5.8019	5.9753	6.1533
6	6.2135	6.4343	6.6625	6.8983	7.1420	7.3938	7.6540
7	7.2857	7.5830	7.8923	8.2142	8.5491	8.8975	9.2598
8	8.3685	8.7546	9.1591	9.5828	10.0266	10.4913	10.9780
9	9.4622	9.9497	10.4639	11.0061	11.5779	12.1808	12.8164
10	10.5668	11.1687	11.8078	12.4864	13.2068	13.9716	14.7836
15	16.2579	17.6393	19.1569	20.8245	22.6575	24.6725	26.8881
20	22.2392	24.7833	27.6765	30.9692	34.7193	38.9927	43.8652
25	28.5256	32.6709	37.5530	43.3117	50.1135	58.1564	67.6765
30	35.1327	41.3794	49.0027	58.3283	69.7608	83.8017	101.0730
35	42.0769	50.9944	62.2759	76.5983	94.8363	118.1209	147.9135
40	49.3752	61.6100	77.6633	98.8265	126.8398	164.0477	213.6096
Year	8.00%	9.00%	10.00%	11.00%	12.00%	14.00%	15.00%
1	1.0800	1.0900	1.1000	1.1100	1.1200	1.1400	1.1500
2	2.2464	2.2781	2.3100	2.3421	2.3744	2.4396	2.4725
3	3.5061	3.5731	3.6410	3.7097	3.7793	3.9211	3.9934
4	4.8666	4.9847	5.1051	5.2278	5.3528	5.6101	5.7424
5	6.3359	6.5233	6.7156	6.9129	7.1152	7.5355	7.7537
6	7.9228	8.2004	8.4872	8.7833	9.0890	9.7305	10.0668
7	9.6366	10.0285	10.4359	10.8594	11.2997	12.2328	12.7268
8	11.4876	12.0210	12.5795	13.1640	13.7757	15.0853	15.7858
9	13.4866	14.1929	14.9374	15.7220	16.5487	18.3373	19.3037
10	15.6455	16.5603	17.5312	18.5614	19.6546	22.0445	23.3493
15	29.3243	32.0034	34.9497	38.1899	41.7533	49.9804	54.7175
20	49.4229	55.7645	63.0025	71.2651	80.6987	103.7684	117.8101
25	78.9544	92.3240	108.1818	126.9988	149.3339	207.3327	244.7120
30	122.3459	148.5752	180.9434	220.9132	270.2926	406.7370	499.9569
35	186.1021	235.1247	298.1268	379.1644	483.4631	790.6729	1013.3457
40	279.7810	368.2917	486.8518	645.8269	859.1424	1529.9086	2045.9539

The following example illustrates the use of the GROWTH OF $1 table. Under the 10% column on the 20-year row, is the number 6.7275. That means $1 grows to $6.73 in 20 years at 10% growth. If you have more than $1 invested, then multiply the factor by the amount of investment. For instance, if you have $25,000 invested for 20 years at 10% growth, the ending amount will be $168,187.50 (6.7275 times $25,000).

The same table illustrates the effects of price inflation. For example, assume inflation is 2% per year for the next 25 years. Under the 2% column on the 25-year row is the number 1.6406. Something that costs $25,000 now will cost ($25,000 times 1.6406) or $41,015 after 25 years.

The following example illustrates the use of the SAVINGS GROWTH table. Under the 12% column on the 5-year row is the number 7.1152. An annual one dollar investment grows to $7.12 in five years assuming 12% compounded growth. In 30 years, the $30 out of pocket contributions grow to $270.29. If you invest $3700 each year for 30 years at 12% growth, the result is $1,000,082.62 ($3700 times 270.2926).

You can also use the above table to calculate the annual amount required to reach a future goal. For instance, you may want to know the annual investment required to accumulate $1,000,000 in 30 years assuming 10% return. Across from 30 years in the 10% column is the number 180.9434. Divide $1,000,000 by 180.9434 to get the annual contribution necessary to reach the goal. The answer is $5,527.

How Much Will $1 Million Be Worth in Today's Dollars at Age 65?

Your age now	25	30	35	40	45	50
Inflation rate						
1%	671,650	705,914	741,923	779,768	819,544	861,350
2%	452,890	500,028	552,071	609,531	672,971	743,010
3%	306,560	355,383	411,987	477,608	553,676	641,860
4%	208,290	253,415	308,319	375,117	456,387	555,260
5%	142,050	181,290	231,377	295,303	376,889	481,020
6%	97,222	130,105	174,110	232,999	311,805	417,270

How Much Savings Do You Need at Age 65?

Assumptions: Inflation before and after retirement is 4%. Investment return before retirement is 10% and after retirement is 7%. Account is depleted at age 90.

Your age now	25	30	35	40	45	50
Total Goal	3.0 mil	2.5 mil.	2.1 mil.	1.7 mil.	1.4 mil.	1.1 mil.
Annual Goal	6,890	9,248	12,524	17,217	24,300	36,004

The above table shows how much money you would need to retire at age 65 with an inflation adjusted income of $35,000. Inflation adjusted income means that each year the income payout would increase to keep up with estimated inflation. Although the above numbers seem quite high, the table is actually conservative. If the value of the portfolio did not increase 7% each year after age 65, income payout would have to be reduced in order to prevent the account from becoming exhausted before age 90.

Appendix E

Dollar Cost Averaging
$200 per month investment

Month	Price Per Share	Number of Shares	Total No. of Shares	Total Amount Invested	Average Cost Per Share
1	$16.00	12.50	12.50	$200.00	$16.00
2	$18.00	11.11	23.61	$400.00	$16.94
3	$20.00	10.00	33.61	$600.00	$17.85
4	$14.00	14.29	47.90	$800.00	$16.70
5	$13.00	15.38	63.28	$1,000.00	$15.80
6	$16.00	12.50	75.78	$1,200.00	$15.84
Average price per share = (16+18+20+14+13+16) / 6 = 16.16					

Index

About the Author

J. B. Davis is a Certified Financial Planner® licensee and a Chartered Mutual Fund Counselor℠ designee. He has a Master's Degree in Business Administration (Finance Major) from The University of Texas at Austin. In his first job after getting his MBA, J. B. worked as a trust investments officer for a large East Coast bank. In that job, he analyzed common stocks as investments in trust accounts. Subsequently, J. B. worked as a Certified Public Accountant in the tax department of a national CPA firm. He then worked eleven years in the headquarters of a large mutual funds organization in Houston, TX.

J. B. is now president of a financial retirement education firm which helps educate corporate employees about personal finance, specializing in 401(k) plans and IRAs.

Business Owners: You can order copies for your employees.

Need Great Gifts for Friends? See Quantity Discounts Below.

This book can be ordered through your bookstore, or you can charge it by calling 1-800-431-1579.

MasterCard	Visa	Discover	American Express

Quantity Discounts

Quantities of 10 to 99 shipped to one location are $10.50 for each book, with no shipping charges within the continental U.S. For shipments to Texas, price per book for 10 or more books is $11.37 including sales tax. To get this discount, send check or money order to Galaxy Publishing Co., P.O. Box 10035, Houston, TX 77206. Charge card not accepted for this special discount. For greater discounts on more than 99 books, please call 1-800-338-7153 or write to the publisher at the above address. Additional information on this book is at www.401kmillionaire.com

Notes

Ordering Information

(Over)

Business Owners: You can order copies for your employees.

Need Great Gifts for Friends? See Quantity Discounts Below.

This book can be ordered through your bookstore, or you can charge it by toll free telephone number.
To charge by phone, call 1-800-431-1579.

| MasterCard | Visa | Discover | American Express |

Quantity Discounts

Quantities of 10 to 99 shipped to one location are $10.50 for each book, with no shipping charges within the continental U.S. For shipments to Texas, price per book for 10 or more books is $11.37 including sales tax. To get this discount, send check or money order to Galaxy Publishing Co., P.O. Box 10035, Houston, TX 77206. Charge card not accepted for this special discount. For greater discounts on more than 99 books, please call 1-800-338-7153 or write to the publisher at the above address. Additional information on this book is at www.401kmillionaire.com